From Horror to Transcendence

MASCOT BOOKS
an imprint of Amplify Publishing Group

www.mascotbooks.com

From Horror to Transcendence: How I Lost Everything in the Material World, Then Found Everything Within

Cover photo by Jennifer Compton Photography

For more information, please contact:
Mascot Books, an imprint of Amplify Publishing Group
620 Herndon Parkway, Suite 320
Herndon, VA 20170
info@mascotbooks.com

Library of Congress Control Number: 2022919938

CPSIA Code: PRV0223A
ISBN-13: 978-1-63755-329-9

Printed in the United States

This book is dedicated to Ralph Baker Shelton III, known to his family and friends as Trey. I think about you often and miss you always.

It is also dedicated to my parents, Gail and Jerry Curnutt, and to my brother, Kelly Curnutt, who have always been there with love and support.

FROM HORROR TO TRANSCENDENCE

How I Lost Everything in the Material World, Then Found Everything Within

Kevin Curnutt with Tim Madigan

PROLOGUE

The date was January 25, 1981. It was Super Bowl Sunday. My best friend, Trey Shelton, and I had been to church and were now loose on dirt bikes, roaring across the hilly, wooded acres that belonged to Trey's family on the rural outskirts of Arlington, Texas. My name is Kevin Curnutt, and I was thirteen years old.

I will always remember the vision of Trey riding ahead of me, the noise and speed and euphoria of that afternoon, the wind running through my shaggy red hair, the warm winter sun washing down. That would be my last vision of an idyllic young life—Trey crossing a shallow stream on his bike and disappearing over a hill. Because of the loud whining of the bike engines, I didn't hear the shotgun blast ahead of me.

Instead, the next thing I heard was the concerned voices of my parents and my older brother, Kelly; the unrecognizable voices of doctors and nurses; the rhythmic beeping of medical equipment. I eventually managed to put together that I was lying in a hospital bed. Riotous thoughts began to push through the fog of what had been a two-week coma: Where am I? Why am I here? What happened?

In the early moments of my awakening, there was also the terrifying realization that, try as I might, I could not move my arms or my legs, not even a fraction of an inch, nor could I utter a word or make a sound of any kind.

The year was 2005. By then I was in my late thirties. My once pudgy body was long and lean and folded each day into a high-tech wheelchair. It had been nearly a decade since I'd made the decision to abandon a grueling rehabilitation program called patterning, which my family and I had so desperately hoped would put me back on my feet again. Hundreds of devoted volunteers had been part of that herculean effort, which went on for nearly fifteen years, but my hard work and their heroics could not alter the bitter reality that I eventually had to accept: I would be a quadriplegic for the rest of my life because of the shotgun pellet that tore through my brain on that sunny winter day in 1981.

After the patterning was finished, I had focused my energies on trying to make a life for myself, however limited it might be. Voice recognition technology made it possible for me to work as a computer programmer, design websites, and trade stocks. I hit the craps and blackjack tables in Las Vegas. I rolled down the River Walk in San Antonio. Thanks to a large and devoted circle of friends, I enjoyed a lively social life—dinners out, barhopping, movies, and concerts. For the better part of a decade, I felt something resembling happiness.

But it turned out that the inner furies had just been biding their time. At first they visited only in the darkness of the night, which is why I began to dread the time when my caregiver lifted me from my wheelchair into bed and my parents came in to say good night and turn off the lights. I was alone again in the one-room apartment built onto the back of our home. Once more I was at the mercy of the same questions that tumbled relentlessly across my mind and heart night after night, keeping me from sleep, driving me deeper and deeper into despair.

I could not stop thinking about all the things I would never be able to do—drive a car, lift a fork, and so many other things. I was convinced that no woman would ever want to marry a man in my condition. I would never be a father. All because of the madman with a shotgun on that sunny winter day so long ago, the man who killed Trey and left me paralyzed. More and more as the months of 2005 wore on, I was consumed by the injustice and hopelessness of it all.

In another life so long ago, I had been a happy, curious, red-haired kid who had never been kissed. A good kid, like Trey. So why had this happened? Alone in the dark, I kept searching for some explanation, some rationale behind the evil. I continued to be tortured by the reality that, for as long as I lived, others would have to lift a straw to my lips, help me pee, put me to bed.

Why me?

Why Trey?

What kind of world would do this to me?

Ultimately, by the summer and early fall of 2005, the furies began to consume the daytime too. My parents sensed the change. I was just tired, I replied when they asked me about it. But it was so much more than that. It felt like a vise was being tightened on my head. I couldn't flee or physically lash out, trapped as I was in that lifeless shell, so I sat alone in my wheelchair, hour after hour, staring at the walls of my room.

More and more I imagined myself on a long dock at a nearby lake, rolling my motorized chair toward the end of it, then tumbling into the water, and then, finally, peace . . .

CHAPTER ONE

My story begins in windblown West Texas, in a modest home at the edge of Lubbock. I will always remember the wind and the grit from my early childhood in the 1960s, tumbleweeds stacked as high as the backyard fence. My brother, Kelly, was two years older than me. We built forts out of what we called tummy weed. Our mother, Gail Curnutt, had taught elementary school but was taking several years off to raise Kelly and me. Our dad, Jerry, was an Internal Revenue Service agent. The four of us took summer camping trips. Our family shared supper every night. Such were the seemingly mundane details of my early life, but when nearly everything is taken away, nothing is ever mundane again—nothing is trivial.

In 1972 the IRS transferred my dad to Dallas, and our parents built a spacious home on the outskirts of suburban Arlington. I was five years old when we moved, a pudgy youngster with an independent streak who never cared about being one of the popular kids in school and who enjoyed being alone. I loved animals and thought someday I might become a veterinarian. That or a chef, because cooking was another early passion. My mom spent hours in the kitchen teaching me to follow recipes for Rice Krispies bars or chocolate chip cookies, which I baked myself and took to school.

Not until seventh grade did some of life's more difficult realities begin to intrude. As an overweight, red-haired boy, I was an easy target for the bullies at Young Junior High. Kids called me Puffy because of my weight. There were several calls from the school to my parents about discipline issues. My grades suffered. But I never let on to my parents about the bullying, and in any event, life changed dramatically when I transferred to Gunn Junior High for eighth grade. My older brother was a freshman there, a top student, a star athlete, good with the girls, and one of the most popular kids in his class. Kelly was known at Gunn as Big C. I, of course, became Little C. With Kelly around, bullies wouldn't dare mess with Little C.

Years later, with all the pain to come, remembering those few months at Gunn, I would find it hard to believe a kid could be so happy. Whenever Kelly's buddies hung out at our house, which was often, I was invited to join them. I also made many of my own friends at Gunn, most of them guys on the eighth-grade football team. I was one of the offensive linemen, who the coach called "the pie eaters."

Trey Shelton was a pie eater, too, a boy whose thirst for adventure and sense of humor matched my own.

Trey's full name was Ralph Baker Shelton III. He was the son of a former Arlington city councilman who was a leading real estate developer and an accomplished horseman. Fourteen-year-old Trey also became one of the top cutting horse riders for his age in the nation. Trey and his dad, Ralph, would drive across the Southwest to cutting horse competitions, pulling a horse trailer behind their pickup, listening to Willie Nelson and Richard Pryor, talking about everything, or just riding in companionable silence. In the fall of 1980, I was invited to ride along on a few of those trips.

Trey's family owned several hilly acres in southwest Arlington, wooded land with a large house, a stable for their horses, and fenced corrals. Bowen Road ran along the east side of the Shelton property. It was just across Bowen that Ralph had donated land for Rush Creek Christian Church, a new congregation founded by a minister named Dick Lord. My brother and Jimmy Lord, one of the preacher's sons, were close friends, which is the major reason my family came to be members at Rush Creek.

Life was good for our family. My dad's career flourished. My mom loved her teaching job. Our home was always full of Kelly's friends. After a hard year, I was happy and content. In early January 1981, we took our first ski trip to Colorado.

The only real hint of the horror to come was on a Saturday morning that winter, when my dad picked us up at Trey's house. We piled into the back seat, and as he drove, my dad overheard Trey tell me that a few days before, on New Year's Eve, one of his father's prized cutting horses had been mysteriously shot and killed in the family's barn. This did not really register with me, and I do not remember it. But my dad later recalled that upon hearing Trey say this, he was stunned, but for some reason he decided not to say anything, and he didn't think of it again until after the worst had happened. For the rest of his life, he would be haunted by the fact he didn't follow up.

I often spent the night at Trey's house in those days. Saturday night, January 24, 1981, was the first time Trey slept over at my place. Trey and I were having such a good time talking, laughing, and cutting up late into the night that my dad finally had to poke his head in and tell us to pipe down and go to sleep because we had to be up early the next morning for church.

The next day, most of America prepared for the late-afternoon kickoff of the Super Bowl, featuring the Oakland Raiders and the Philadelphia Eagles, but no one in our family was particularly interested in the game. My parents got Trey and I up for church, but Kelly stayed at home because he had come down with a slight cold. After church services, my parents, Trey, and I went back to my house to eat lunch. My parents, who were excellent country-and-western dancers, had volunteered to teach dance lessons to the Rush Creek youth group later that afternoon. Kelly, Trey, and I belonged to the youth group, but Kelly was sick, and I decided I could dance well enough already. In fact, I thought I was a *very* good dancer, so what did I need with a beginners' class in country-and-western dancing? Hanging out at Trey's place seemed a much better option. My parents did not argue. After lunch, my mom dropped us off at the Sheltons' before driving back across Bowen Road to join my dad at the church.

Arriving back at Trey's house, we visited together and talked to his sisters (Heather and Wendy) and his mom (Roselin). It was Heather's birthday, and she was having a birthday party that afternoon. Trey and I hung around the house for a little while, and then we decided to go for a ride. I didn't own a motorcycle of any kind, but Trey had a small red Honda dirt bike, and a good friend of his who lived nearby had left his bigger Yamaha dirt bike there at Trey's house.

I was relatively new to riding motorcycles, so of course I thought this was great fun. To feel the power of the dirt bike, riding up and down the trails and over the creek, and exploring new areas was, I thought, the best feeling ever! Could I be any happier, or feel any more exhilarated? I sure didn't think so!

Country music and teenage laughter filtered out from the Rush Creek youth area, where my parents taught fifteen teenagers the Texas two-step. My mom was dancing with a boy named Chris Bailey, a good friend of mine, when a police officer entered the room, speaking first with my dad.

"Mr. Curnutt came over to where we were dancing and tapped Gail on the shoulder and pulled her away," Chris remembered decades later. "They walked to the front door, and I saw her put her face in her hands. I knew something was wrong, and then the word spread pretty fast. We all knew that there was a shooting across the street."

Minutes later a second officer brought additional details. He reported that two boys had been shot off their dirt bikes in the woods across Bowen. My parents knew that was the Shelton property. They also knew that was how Trey and I had planned to spend the afternoon.

"Oh my God," my dad said.

He caught my mom when she fainted.

"We knew Kevin and Trey were involved," Chris Bailey remembered. "I didn't know Trey, but I knew of him. We sat there as the whole thing unfolded for what seemed like hours. We saw police activity; the police cars were all over the street and the church parking lot. I remember being unbelievably upset, crying uncontrollably. My dad was finally able to pick me up. When we got home, we were switching the television back and forth, watching all the news channels, and it seemed each story was different. You didn't know what was accurate and what wasn't. One report said there were two dead. Another said the shooter was dead; another said the shooter was in custody. It was a really a long night."

In the minutes after it happened, other adults arrived at the church to look after the horrified members of the youth group. My dad headed outside and walked toward Bowen, seeing the crush of emergency vehicles with their flashing lights and the flurry of police activity.

This is really bad, my dad thought.

The next thing he remembered was driving with my mom in shocked silence to an Arlington hospital. For the first but hardly the last time, my parents wondered if they had gotten caught up in a particularly bad dream.

Richard Tiedemann was thirty-two, a Princeton-educated aerospace engineer who worked for a local defense contractor. But at the time the shooting occurred, neighbors in the scattered homes surrounding Tiedemann's house knew him only as an odd and unfriendly man who lived in a small white house deep in the trees off Bowen Road. He kept his front gate closed and locked. No one else was ever seen coming or going. Neighbors occasionally noticed him working in his yard or tinkering with a sailboat. He had surrounded his property with a barbed wire fence, and on the few occasions he spoke with his neighbors, it was to remind them in no uncertain terms to stay on their own side of it.

"He moved into the house thinking that he was moving out into the country," one neighbor said later. "He didn't move far enough."

He certainly wasn't the only area resident annoyed by the noise of dirt bikes. The motorcycles were everywhere in that rural part of Arlington, where there were probably more horses than houses. The ying-ying of the machines was a near constant sound after school, on weekends, and in the summer, but most residents resigned themselves to the din. Tiedemann never did. In the fall of 1980, he filed a noise complaint with the Arlington Police Department but was apparently unsatisfied with the response.

One sunny autumn day of that year, a woman named Kathy Strong heard the bikes as they made several loud passes past her place, racing by on the rough trail that crossed a creek and climbed a hill before running into Bowen Road. The trail was on a long finger of property belonging to the Shelton family, and it ran between Strong's home and the fence bordering Richard Tiedemann's land.

Strong was irked on the days the noise interfered with the afternoon nap of her five-year-old son, Cody. But that day Cody was happily playing in the driveway while his mother watered plants on a second-story deck facing Tiedemann's property.

She looked toward the source of the noise, expecting to see the bikes, but instead saw her neighbor. Tiedemann had slipped through the barbed wire fence and onto the trail and was crouched behind a tree with a long-handled shovel cocked over his shoulder. It was obvious he planned to ambush the bikers when they crossed the creek and motored past him.

You idiot, Strong thought.

She rushed downstairs, grabbed Cody, and hurried him inside, then watched as Tiedemann, who had apparently got tired of waiting, slipped back through his fence and trudged back toward his home. His tendencies toward violence would intensify. After Trey and I were shot, investigators concluded that on a night a few months earlier it was Tiedemann who snuck onto the Shelton property and killed Ralph Shelton's quarter horse with a shotgun. Ballistics determined that the same weapon he had used to kill the animal would soon be used for far more sinister purposes.

On Super Bowl Sunday, just after 3:00 p.m., Kathy Strong again heard the familiar whine of the bikes and then another, much different sound that she immediately recognized as a gunshot. It seemed to come from right outside her door, so she dropped a basket of laundry and rushed to find Cody, who was on his tricycle in the driveway.

When she looked toward the trail, she saw a yellow dirt bike on its side, its wheels still spinning. Trey was sprawled on the ground a few feet away, motionless. Strong thought at first that he had taken an accidental spill, but then she saw Tiedemann, dressed in a red plaid shirt and blue jeans, in a kneeling position, holding a shotgun in both hands like he was hunting and poised to fire again. He stared at the fallen boy as if in a trance. Cody ran up to his mother.

"Mommy, Mommy. That man just shot that boy."

"You idiot!" Strong screamed at Tiedemann.

She shoved Cody toward the open garage of her sister's home, which was next door to her own, terrified she or her son would be shot as they fled. When her seven-year-old niece, Kadee, came out of the house, Strong yelled for her to get back inside. Then she heard another bike approaching down the trail. I was headed that way, totally unaware of the mortal peril that lay in wait.

Strong ran toward the noise, screaming to try to warn me, but she realized she could not be heard over the roaring of the bike's engine, that there was no way to prevent what was about to happen. Tiedemann, who was still kneeling, raised his shotgun and fired, hitting me in the head from close range. I tumbled to the ground, unconscious, my red dirt bike coming to rest on top of me.

Tiedemann lowered his weapon and stood. He calmly looked at Trey and me before slipping back through his fence and walking slowly toward his home.

Mike Yantis was a rookie patrol officer with the Arlington Police Department. Early in his shift, the words "shots fired" came over his radio, followed by a street address that was only a few blocks from his location. Yantis sped in that direction. Just before he rolled up, he heard an even more ominous message: "Two gunshot victims and a possible sniper situation in progress."

Kathy Strong, deeply shaken, was waiting outside her home and pointed to the place in the woods where Trey and I and our motorbikes were lying. Then she pointed at the white house visible through the trees. That was where the shooter lived. Strong told Yantis the man was probably still inside.

The young officer drew his weapon and hurried to Trey and me, keeping an eye on the white house. He got to Trey first. My husky friend was dressed in a short-sleeved blue shirt and lay on his back in the grass and leaves, not breathing. A few feet away, Yantis saw me under my bike, unconscious, bleeding from a head wound and convulsing. He then pulled the bike off me as an ambulance and detectives Tommy Ingram and Ruben Puente pulled up on Bowen Road.

"Hang in there. I'll be right back with you," Yantis told me. "I'm going to get help."

Ingram and Puente were both just twenty-six years old themselves, having risen quickly through the ranks of the Arlington Police Department to become investigators. That Sunday the partners had been following leads in a homicide case and were about to wrap things up for the day, when the call came over the radio. They raced across town and saw Yantis's patrol car parked on the side of Bowen Road.

Yantis met the detectives, pointing through the trees to where Trey and I were lying in the grass and dead leaves. The gunman was thought to be in the white house visible through the foliage.

"There was kind of a drop-off from Bowen Road down into a little gully," Ingram remembered decades later in an interview with Tim Madigan. "It was wooded, and there was some brush, but I could see a kid actually laying down there. So we pulled out our guns and headed toward him."

Ingram and Puente immediately concluded the bullet wound to the back of Trey's head had been fatal.

"We could see Kevin maybe twenty yards to thirty yards away, on a little bit of a rise, laying there, but he was moving," Ingram remembered. "We could tell that he had a grave head injury, but he was still alive."

The detectives stationed Yantis behind a small outbuilding, where he had a clear view of the shooter's home. Puente stayed with me while Ingram sprinted to meet the paramedics.

"The ambulance attendants would not go down into an area where an active gunman was, so I made a deal with them," Ingram remembered. "I would drive my unmarked car down in there and provide a shield for them so they could carry the gurney to get to Kevin. That's what we did. The car provided a physical barrier so they could get to Kevin and get him on the gurney. On the way back, they were struggling with the gurney, so I jumped out of the car and grabbed the gurney, and between the three of us, we were able to get it up the hill and back to the road."

One of the paramedics said my condition looked hopeless.

"He won't last the drive to the hospital," the paramedic said.

"Get him there anyway," Ingram replied.

Puente had remained with Trey's body, planning to carry it from the crime scene himself after I had been evacuated. But then he heard Yantis yelling, warning of movement near the house. The detective took cover behind a tree and waited, looking over at the fallen boy. When he spoke of it thirty-nine years later, Puente began to weep.

"I just didn't want him to be alone," he said.

Officers from the APD Tactical Unit surrounded Tiedemann's home. Just before dark, his front door opened, and Tiedemann stepped out onto the porch in plain view, carrying a shotgun down along one leg. He walked down the steps and through the dusk to his detached garage, seemingly oblivious to the phalanx of officers and the guns pointed in his direction. Police heard Tiedemann talking to himself.

He briefly poked around inside his garage, came back out into the twilight, circled the outbuilding as if looking for something, and then casually made his way back toward his house. When he got to his porch, Tiedemann turned and leveled his weapon, firing two shots toward the police.

"Green light" came over police radios.

At that signal, the tactical unit unleashed a fusillade of gunfire. Tiedemann fell and began to scream, crawling toward the door of his home, leaving a broad trail of blood across his porch, but he managed to get inside. When he ignored attempts to contact him, police launched a tear-gas canister through a window, and the home caught fire.

By then the sun had gone down completely, and it was very dark in the woods. The front door opened, and Tiedemann stood in the doorway, backlit by the fire. He fell onto the porch and fired again into the night. Police responded with another flurry of gunfire, until the man on the porch fell still. Tiedemann was dead by the time officers reached him, lying next to his 12-gauge shotgun.

When the fire was extinguished, detectives searched Tiedemann's home for a motive for the horrifying attack but found none. He just didn't like the noise.

CHAPTER TWO

In a waiting room at Arlington Community Hospital, my parents watched a police officer approach Trey's mother, Roselin, and break the news to her that Trey was dead. Roselin was with a friend that day because Trey's father, Ralph, had been out of town when the shooting happened. My mom was devastated for Trey and his family, but she was also relieved because I was probably still alive. Her relief was momentary. A few minutes later, an emergency room physician came out to speak with my parents.

"I have to be honest with you," the doctor told them. "Your son has been mortally wounded and is unconscious. He won't know you're here."

A shotgun pellet had entered my brain at the right temple and come out the other side. Death was expected at any moment, the doctor said. I almost certainly would not live through the night. The doctor discouraged my parents from seeing me. My mom bent and absently used her tear-sodden Kleenex to wipe my blood from the doctor's shoes.

"We're going in," she told him.

My parents were led to the room where I lay in a coma, my head wrapped in bandages, my young face swollen. I had been wearing blue jeans and a down vest that afternoon. My mom would remember how feathers from the vest were scattered across the bloody floor.

My brother, Kelly, arrived at the hospital, driven by his girlfriend's mother. He and my parents embraced and wept in a hospital corridor. My family met Dr. Carlos Acosta, a neurosurgeon, who told them that he needed to operate immediately to stop the bleeding and remove bone fragments. If I did survive, the surgeon cautioned, it would probably be in some form of vegetative state.

The vigil began. The shooting dominated the local television news that night, and scores of friends began arriving at the hospital. My dad wandered past a waiting-room television and heard a reporter say both boys had been killed. Dad rushed back to the intensive care unit to make sure the report was wrong, seeing that his son still clung to life.

"The only way I can describe it is to say it was as if I had spent a lot of time looking directly into the sun," my dad said years later.

My mom signed legal documents giving permission for my organs to be harvested for transplant.

"At first the idea bothered me a great deal, but then I began to think maybe it would be a way part of him could live," she remembered. "At that time I think we were resigning ourselves to his death. I remember looking at the form and the list of things it had—eyes, liver, heart, and skin. The thought of someone else with Kevin's skin really bothered me. I kept trying to imagine someone with his freckles."

But I was still alive when the sun rose the next day, and the next. When the doctors removed me from a ventilator, they were surprised I was able to breathe on my own. That meant I was almost certain to survive.

"Now, what would the quality of survival be?" wondered Acosta, the neurosurgeon. Given the path of the shotgun pellet, the surgeon still believed I would be deeply compromised.

A week passed. Diane Salazar, a nurse in the intensive care unit, told my mom that my blood pressure spiked when friends and family entered my room, which was a hopeful sign. My parents took turns talking, reading, and singing to me.

Two weeks after the shooting, with me still in a coma, my mom and Diane Salazar were chatting at my bedside.

"Kevin, I bet you'd like some ice cream," Diane said.

"Oh no, he's a pizza man," Mom said.

She told the nurse about my recent visit to Chuck E. Cheese, and how her husky son had gotten stuck in a play cubicle meant for younger children.

"Kevin, you must really have been a sight," the nurse said. "Your butt must have been a foot in the air."

What happened next was unmistakable. I smiled and laughed out loud.

My mom and the nurse embraced and wept.

I had experienced my first moments of consciousness well before anyone else knew I was awake. They were mere glimpses at first. My eyesight was hazy and out of focus, but I could hear voices at my bedside and the sound of medical equipment. I fell back into the coma before I could begin to attempt to figure out where I was and why.

The periods of consciousness became longer and longer each time I awoke, but I still seemed to be caught up in some bizarre nightmare. Just moments before, or so it seemed to me, I had been riding dirt bikes with Trey, and the very next thing I knew, I was waking up in a hospital. What was going on?

I could make out the voices of my family and people I assumed to be doctors and nurses. Their conversations were clearly about me and not at all encouraging. Everyone sounded serious and sad and spoke of me like I couldn't hear them, as if I wasn't there.

I wanted to scream, "I'm in here," but for some strange reason, my voice wouldn't cooperate. My arms and legs wouldn't cooperate either. I had never consciously thought about using my voice or my limbs before. Who does? If I wanted to speak, I just spoke. If I wanted to move my arms or legs, I just moved them. Now, when I tried to speak or move my arms and legs, nothing at all happened. It was all so bizarre, and absolutely terrifying. I was trapped in a completely lifeless body.

Then I heard my mom mention that day in Chuck E. Cheese, which I thought was funny, and I must have conveyed that somehow, because Mom and the nurse reacted so dramatically, hugging each other, laughing, and speaking in voices that were elated rather than sad.

My dad soon joined in the celebration. I listened as my mom told him the story about Chuck E. Cheese and about my miraculous chuckle. Kelly showed up not long after, having been brought from school. Doctors and nurses came in. There was a new urgency in everyone.

"Kevin, can you squeeze my hand?"

Once more I concentrated and gave it my every effort, but I couldn't squeeze at all.

"Kevin, blink once if you can hear me."

I blinked. That was a relief! I could blink with no effort at all!

The joyous impact of that simple act, blinking, was something I will never forget. There were more hugs and happy weeping at my bedside. After all the terror and confusion, with one blink I was back in touch with the world. Everyone knew for certain I was in there. They knew I was not a vegetable. They knew I was Kevin.

I remember dozing off, exhausted but relieved. When I awoke, I saw my parents and the blurry faces of some friends who had come to visit. I grinned and blinked at them. But where was Trey? Why was my best friend not among the visitors? I had no way of knowing, just as I had no way to ask for a sip of water or to tell my family I was freezing or to ask why in the world I was in a hospital to begin with.

Kelly had an idea. On a piece of paper, he wrote out the alphabet in large block letters and held the paper close to my face, asking me to spell out a word by blinking, letter by letter. Kelly got most of the way through the alphabet, pointing to each letter. I still had not blinked by the time we reached S, and Kelly started to think his plan was not working. But he kept going, and I seemed to blink at T. Kelly pointed again just to make sure. There was no doubt about it. I blinked at T.

We started over at A, once more taking the letters in order. I blinked when Kelly got to H.

T-H-I-R-S-T-Y.

Another celebration broke out in the intensive care unit. My mom lifted a straw to my lips.

Kelly began another word.

C-O-L-D.

A nurse brought a blanket, and I was comforted with the warmth it brought to me.

We started a third word.

T-R-E-Y?

My parents looked at each other. They knew their son needed to know what happened, so they took turns talking, telling me about the horrible way that beautiful winter afternoon had ended a few weeks before, how a madman shot us off our dirt bikes because he didn't like the noise. They told me that Trey had died. I was devastated. Heartbroken. Trey was gone? Forever? It was hard to believe. Impossible to believe. I squeezed my eyes shut, and my tears flowed uncontrollably.

My mom started to pray the moment she learned about the shooting. She never stopped.

"Dear Lord, please let him live."

Within a few days of the shooting, that prayer had been answered.

"Dear Lord, if you would just allow him to wake up."

"Dear Lord, if he could just be able to think and to understand that we love him."

"Dear Lord, if he can just see and hear and communicate."

One by one, miracle followed upon miracle. She kept praying.

"Dear Lord, please let Kevin walk again."

My mom was certain God would answer that prayer too. She believed that for years. We all did.

My doctors had never seen an injury like mine, and they were amazed at how the shotgun pellet had penetrated my brain with such precision. I would have died if the trajectory of the projectile had varied by just a fraction of an inch. It was astounding that it had spared my cognition, hearing, and much of my vision but had devastated the part of my brain that controlled motor functions. The resulting paralysis would probably be permanent, but I had already beaten such long odds by surviving, so who knew for sure?

A few weeks after I awoke from the coma, I was stable enough to be transferred to a rehabilitation hospital in nearby Dallas. Eyeglasses helped to clear my vision, and after several months I could see well enough without them. Learning to speak again was much more difficult. For weeks, all I could do was grunt. In daily sessions with a speech therapist, I was taught to form sounds by holding my mouth and tongue in a certain way. It took a year for me to relearn how to speak, word by word.

Later, in the summer of 1981, I was referred to Craig Rehabilitation Hospital in Englewood, Colorado, a nationally known center for the treatment of spinal cord and traumatic brain injuries.

"They will teach you how to walk again," Acosta, the Arlington neurosurgeon, told me before we left for Colorado.

That was not to be. I returned to Texas after a two-month stay with many new coping skills, but we were told my paralysis would be permanent.

"The people telling us these things were highly trained professionals for whom we had a great deal of respect," my dad said years later. "But we simply could not accept their conclusions. We had no idea when or how, but we felt strongly that the day would come when Kevin would be able to walk again. We just had to keep searching and praying that we might find the way."

"Courage and perseverance," Acosta said. "Another set of parents would have sent him to a nursing home."

The answer to my family's prayers seemed to come about a year after the shooting. One day, while driving to work, my dad heard a news report on the radio about research to help children with brain injuries. He was on the telephone minutes later. His inquiries eventually led to a place called the Institutes for the Achievement of Human Potential, located in Philadelphia. Researchers there were exploring whether a program called patterning could restore motor function to people paralyzed by brain injuries of all kinds.

In March 1982, my parents, Kelly, and I made the trip to Philadelphia. There we had meetings with the experts, who explained the program's theory.

"The institute operates on the philosophy that a very small portion of the brain controls all the physical movements of the body," Dallas journalist Carlton Stowers later wrote in a *D Magazine* article. "It is possible for another, still healthy part of the brain to be trained to take over the motor function responsibilities of the damaged part through a re-teaching process that sends messages to the limbs. An agonizingly slow process, it is much like training an infant to first crawl, then support his own weight on all fours and finally to stand. In a sense, then, the previously unused portion of a patient's brain has to grow from neurological infancy. Like a new baby that eventually learns to crawl and walk, a paralyzed person could possibly do the same if the lifeless limbs were regularly manipulated to simulate crawling and walking motions."*

It made immediate sense to us.

If a baby can do it, I can do it, I remember thinking.

The bad news was that, to have even a chance at success, I would have to take on a physical regimen that would be enough to overwhelm even the most fit and disciplined professional athlete—ten hours a day, seven days a week, every week of the year. Yet we didn't hesitate, because the alternative was far worse. However challenging it would be,

---

* Carlton Stowers, "The Miracle of Kevin Curnutt," *D Magazine* 12, no. 12 (December 1985).

we knew patterning was my best and probably only chance to walk again.

My dad quit his job at the IRS. My mom retired from teaching. Our family would attempt to make ends meet with savings and financial support from relatives. Our garage was converted into my one-room apartment, which also became the patterning room. Kelly devoted most of his free time to helping me. Still, our family could not do it alone. Patterning required scores of other people—volunteers we recruited from our church, from our friends, and from any other source we could think of.

"This program involves five people moving Kevin's body in crawling motions, the purpose being to [tell the brain], 'This is how it feels to move,'" my parents wrote to prospective volunteers. "Patterning is done for five minutes, fifteen times a day. The quality of the rhythm of the movement is of the utmost importance.

"Before you volunteer, we would like to stress that we are asking quite a bit of you. Patterning is fairly hard work. We try to keep the attitude of an athletic training program."

Yet by the time of my first patterning session in April 1982, more than a hundred names filled my weekly patterning schedule. There were airline pilots, grandmothers, teachers, high school students, and homemakers. Dozens of the volunteers were members of our church, Rush Creek Christian Church, including our minister, Rev. Dick Lord, and a woman named Dot Crofts Mittel.

Dot was the twin sister of the famous singer Dash Crofts (of Seals and Crofts). She had a daughter about my age and lived just down the street from Trey. Her memories of Super Bowl Sunday 1981 would remain vivid for the rest of her life. Dot and her family had had no interest in the big game, because the Dallas Cowboys weren't playing in it, so they decided instead to take in an art exhibition in nearby Fort Worth. Returning to Arlington in the late afternoon, Dot saw an unusual number of cars parked outside the Sheltons' house. A Super Bowl party, she thought. Her telephone rang the moment she stepped inside her door.

A breathless neighbor told her to pull down her blinds because there had been a shooting nearby. Dot gasped when the neighbor said Trey had been killed. I wasn't mentioned at first, but it wasn't long before Dot heard the rest of the story. She and her husband headed for the Arlington hospital to keep vigil with my family and the dozens of others who had shown up.

In the weeks and months to come, Dick Lord provided his congregation with regular updates about my condition and shared the joyous news that I had emerged from my coma. Through the minister, Dot and the others kept up with me and my family during the early months of my recovery. A year after the shooting, Dick put the word out about our need for volunteers. Dot was among the first to sign up.

Her devotion to my recovery lasted more than fourteen years, with Dot committed to a Wednesday-morning patterning shift. The session with four other volunteers began at 9:00 a.m. sharp and lasted exactly an hour and forty minutes. The second team arrived in the afternoon and a third in early evening. My dad was always there to supervise, instruct, and substitute for any team member who was unable to be there, and my mom was a constant source of inspiration, strength, and caring, whether she subbed in for a sick patterner or just came out to say hi.

"It was wonderful, such a blessing," Dot remembered decades later in an interview with Tim Madigan. "You got to know people so well. The other volunteers became friends forever, and Kevin was such a doll. His mind was still working, and his sense of humor—my gosh, can you imagine having a sense of humor while you're in that condition? But it came out immediately. And his parents were so amazing. I got to know them so well. I felt for them so much. Can you imagine having 102 people in your house every week? But they were always so upbeat and hopeful. We were all just a team."

And Dot was not the only one who dedicated so much time and energy to my recovery. Not by a long shot. Over the years, literally hundreds of volunteers generously gave their time to me, without asking for anything.

A family video from January 6, 1984, shows me, a still-stocky boy, suspended from a harness as volunteers moved my arms and legs back and forth, one person on each limb, in a crawling motion. When lowered to the ground, I could support myself on my hands and knees and even move a couple of inches on my own. The video shows volunteers lifting me from the harness onto a table, where I gripped a metal bar and managed to lift a light weight over my head, a feat that seemed miraculous. The session is filled with banter and laughter. Each volunteer donned one of my ballcaps that had been hanging on the wall of my room, and they put one on my head too.

A year later, in 1985, a woman who witnessed a patterning session wrote, "The boy's brightness seemed to set the room aglow. Instead of an emaciated invalid, I met an alert, physically attractive young man whose muscle tone seemed amazing for one who had been paralyzed for three years. I secretly wondered at the ability he had developed to be able to trust so completely in so many people."

That same year, writer Carlton Stowers got wind of the story unfolding in the converted garage in Arlington. His story in *D Magazine* recounted the tragedy and horror of Super Bowl Sunday 1981, my miraculous survival, and the relentless effort of so many to put me back on my feet. Stowers wrote:

> To the casual observer, the progress would seem minimal. Kevin still can't walk or even turn the pages of the books he enjoys reading. But he can now crawl on his stomach as far as 1,000 feet a day on the carpeted floor of his room. And while the harness and lift are still used, he is able to support himself on hands and knees. On the afternoon of October 22, he established a new "record" by moving forward on hands and knees nine inches—five inches better than he had ever done before. His balance has also shown marked improvement in recent months.
>
> "The light at the end of the tunnel is getting much brighter," his father says. "Perhaps it's like first learning to ride a

bicycle. Once you get the balance down and get some momentum, you really pick up speed. We're more encouraged than ever now. When you say it, nine inches of movement doesn't sound like that much. But when you stop to think that what he's done is considered medically impossible, it's really something. Really something."

"When you understand he couldn't even hold up his head alone or move an inch along the floor when he started," says volunteer coordinator Dolly Wadlington, "then you realize the amazing progress he's made. There aren't many kids who would have the strength and courage that he has shown day after day. And the attitude of Jerry and Gail is incredible. They know Kevin will walk again one day, and they are devoting themselves to seeing that happen."*

More from Carlton Stowers in his *D Magazine* article:

Today Kevin Curnutt is eighteen years old. Currently a high school senior, he is aware of the time his injury has cost him. Taking just two courses a year now, he is still four credits shy of graduation at a time when most of his friends have gone off to college.

Someday Kevin himself hopes to be a college student. And, if he can fight his way back, he would like to train to

---

* Carlton Stowers, "The Miracle of Kevin Curnutt," *D Magazine* 12, no. 12 (December 1985).

become a pilot. His dreams are still intact. Despite the fact that he cannot feed or clothe himself, that he has to be lifted from his bed and carried to his specially designed shower and that a simple desire to sit outside in the sun means being strapped into his wheelchair, Kevin holds firmly to his ambitions.

And he is not bitter about his life.

“There are times when I get frustrated,” he says. “Just keeping on with the program gets hard some days, particularly when I reach a plateau and don’t see much improvement.

“See, everything happens so slow—too slow. There have been times when I wondered if I was really getting any better, but then something always happened to show me that I was and I’d be okay again. It hasn’t been that much of a battle because I know this is what I have to do to get well. I really feel like I’m making progress now. It may take another year, maybe two. But I just have to keep telling myself to be patient.”

On his bedroom wall, near a collection of caps and souvenirs given to him by friends, hangs a photograph of Trey Shelton as an eighth grader. Kevin still thinks of his late friend. But the dreams that once came regularly are gone.

“I used to dream about him a lot,” Kevin says. “Not nightmares, nothing scary. Just dreams. I would dream that I was in the school lunchroom and see him across the room. I would go over to him and say, ‘What are you doing here? I thought you were supposed to be dead.’ Dreams like that. But not anymore. All that’s in the past now.”

Kevin Curnutt is well aware of the time, effort and sacrifice his parents and his brother (who is now a sophomore at University of Texas-Arlington) have made in his behalf.

"I know that Mom and Dad get frustrated at times, just like I do. But they're great. So is Kelly. Lesser people would have quit this program or just taken off somewhere. But they believe in what we're doing, just like I do. They go to bed exhausted every night and then are ready to go again the next morning.

"And they're fun to be around. I'm lucky."

With that he falls silent for a moment.

"Back before I got hurt," he says, "Mom and Dad used to go dancing all the time. They both love to dance. But now, they don't have the time anymore. Sometimes I feel bad about that. I wish sometimes that they could go dancing."

Someday Jerry and Gail Curnutt may go dancing again. But not until their work is done, and Kevin is back on his feet. For them, the miracle is not finished.

The home video was taken on March 14, 1989, four years after Stowers's article was published. It showed me on my hands and padded knees, with Dick Lord and another volunteer on the floor beside me. They encouraged me, now a lanky, red-haired young man, and recorded measurements as I struggled to make my way across the room toward the camera, inch by agonizing inch. It was excruciating to watch. My face was flushed and contorted, and my eyes seemed to roll back into my head from the effort and concentration.

The video is how I remember the struggle of those years. It was just so hard to move, and so utterly exhausting. Not that it was physically painful per se, but I felt as if I were running a marathon every single day of my life. I've always been stubborn. That's one thing that kept me going. I wasn't going to fail. But more importantly, I never forgot that this was my last chance to live a normal life.

One year led to the next. Reporters occasionally stopped by to check on my progress. On September 24, 1991, in a ceremony at Arlington City Hall, Mayor Richard Greene recognized my volunteers, thirty-six of whom were able to attend the ceremony. The volunteers were known as Kevin's Team.

"More than two hundred people have given their time to Kevin. The time frame is almost too long to comprehend," my dad said that night in the council chamber. I sat in a wheelchair nearby, surrounded by my remarkable team. "If it was six months or a year or two years, that's one thing. But this long . . . Our amazement at what they've done is exceeded only by our gratitude. We think it is incomparable, unprecedented. It would be difficult to find this many people who have been committed to a cause this long."

We would continue patterning for another five years.

After a few years, I could make an excruciating lap or two back and forth across my room, creeping on all fours. But I could never support my weight standing up and never got close to attempting a step. It began to dawn on all of us that the ultimate goal, allowing me to walk again and to live an independent life, was beyond reach.

That was difficult to accept for everyone, including Trey's parents, Ralph and Roselin Shelton. They had separated before Trey and I had met and divorced shortly after that, but they had worked on separate patterning teams. Roselin continued to volunteer until shortly before her death in 1996. Trey's dad showed up for his patterning shift almost every Tuesday morning for nine years.

Those difficult mornings became the basis of a close and enduring friendship between Ralph and me. As my team worked to manipulate my arms and legs, Ralph told the latest Aggie joke, talked about his horses, and brought me up to date on his family, but otherwise kept his own heartbreak to himself.

"It never entered my mind not to do what I could do," Ralph said years later. "I would not have been able to live with myself. How could I say that just because I lost something I'm not obliged to help them?"

I never felt sad by the reminder of Trey that Ralph represented every week. If anything, I knew the emotional toll was probably greater on Trey's father, who hated to watch me groan and grimace, day after day, year after year. Ralph could never shake the notion that of the two of us, Trey might have been the lucky one.

"We were grateful that Trey didn't have to put up with what Kevin had to put up with," Ralph said. "I just think it would have been such a difficult thing. You lie there and pattern, knowing that his brain was alive, and his body was dead. You just had a hard time not crying every week and thinking about it when you left."

Ralph watched me grow from a pudgy teenager to a lanky young man. After nine years, he began to show up for patterning less often, blaming the demands of his business.

"What a struggle it was," Ralph recalled. "And for all practical purposes, it wasn't doing much good."

In the spring of 1982, we had all undertaken patterning in the hopes that I could be restored to a normal life, but after fourteen years, the program had become a life unto itself. My dad eventually went back to work for the IRS. My friends graduated from college. Kelly became an attorney and married a kind and beautiful young woman named Mary Tom Cravens. Kelly and Mary Tom had two wonderful sons. Other friends also started families and embarked on successful careers. My life, meanwhile, seemed to be passing me by with every ten-hour day that left me physically and emotionally exhausted. At the rate we were going, it would take a century for me to learn to walk again.

The decision to quit patterning was mine alone. It was a very difficult decision because of the inertia that had built up over the years. With all its challenges, the strict and wearying schedules, the program had been the only life we had known for so long. None of us really knew how we would make the transition to what might come next. But eventually it could be put off no longer. One day, in the fall of 1996, I gathered my parents and my brother together and told them it was time to stop patterning.

"I hate to quit. I hate to admit failure," I remember telling them. "You've done so much for me and put so much into this. I know it will be hard for you, too, but I think it's time to stop patterning. You need a break. I need a break. We *all* need a break from this."

My family was disappointed but also relieved.

"Kevin was ready to get on with his life, and the last few years we had been unable to see much noticeable progress," my dad recalled. "It was time for it to happen. We were all really relieved to do something to get out of this rut, in the sense that we had been doggedly pursuing this and making very little progress for the last seven or eight years. And Kevin wanted to get on to doing a million different things."

I contacted each of the current volunteers, who were unanimously supportive. That led to a winter night in Arlington a few months later. January 9, 1997, nearly sixteen years since Richard Tiedemann had opened fire on two unwitting and defenseless boys. But the horrors of that day were not mentioned, nor really thought of at all, in the back room of a local barbecue joint where Kevin's Team gathered to say goodbye to me and to each other. The evening instead became a celebration of the human spirit. It was a very happy and joyous occasion, filled with thoughts of gratitude, well-wishes, and compassion.

Doris Green and her daughters shared one booth. They had patterned with me every Sunday night for eight years.

“I’ll be over every Sunday, Kevin,” Green said that night. “It’s a habit.”

Airline pilot Marvin Baker sat nearby. He had volunteered from the beginning, as had women like Dot Mittel and Dolly Wadlington.

“I’m a relative newcomer,” Jim Lee said that night. “I’ve only been coming for twelve years. It was my job to make sure Kevin didn’t get too full of himself.”

The red sweater I wore that night matched the color of my full beard. My dad raised a straw to my lips so I could take a sip of a soft drink.

“I want to tell everyone how much I appreciate all you’ve done for me over all these years,” I said to them that night. “I am forever in your debt.”

“You’ve done as much for us,” a man said.

“We feel like your family,” a woman said. “You just thought you were getting rid of us!”

Kevin’s Team laughed together, hugged each other, and eventually dispersed into the winter night. On my next birthday a few months later, I would turn thirty years old.

CHAPTER THREE

The light of a new day spilled into my garage apartment, and the moment I opened my eyes, I began to gird myself for the grueling hours to come. It was the force of long habit. But then relief and euphoria washed over me as I remembered. That day in the fall of 1996, for the first time in nearly fifteen years, was mine and mine alone. Patterning was done and over with. My life was finally my own, to do with what I chose.

During the patterning years, my family and friends had tried to break up the grind and give me a taste of normalcy whenever they could, taking me to browse in bookstores, eat in restaurants, and take in the latest blockbuster movie. A teacher stopped by a few times a week to tutor me, which was how I managed to earn my high school diploma, though two years behind my classmates. But every moment of pleasure and relaxation, every moment of distraction, even if it was just to read a few paragraphs from a book, had to be stolen from the patterning schedule, and the next grueling day always loomed. A different life was almost impossible to imagine. Because of patterning, I had never considered going to college or thought about pursuing a career. Patterning, by necessity, was the sum total of my existence.

But not anymore. After fourteen and a half years, I was free to do anything I wanted to do.

On that first glorious morning, I realized I could doze back off to sleep, which I did, because the first team of volunteers would not be showing up promptly at nine. I would decide when to ask my parents to get me up, bathed, and fed. It was as if I had gotten out of the army.

Not long after I stopped patterning, I hired a personal care attendant who would come in the morning to get me up, showered, dressed, and put into my wheelchair. In the evening, he would come put me in bed. This worked out very well because it eased my parents' life and gave me a much greater sense of independence.

And speaking of greater independence, at that time I also got my first motorized wheelchair. Ever since my injury, I had had to be pushed around in a manual wheelchair. There wasn't ever any point in getting a motorized wheelchair while I was patterning. With my time-consuming physical rehabilitation program, the fancy, expensive new wheelchair would have just sat in a corner of my room for 95 percent of the time. And it would have heightened the temptation of taking days off to go motor around somewhere. I definitely could not afford any distractions from my physical program.

My mom later remembered the years immediately following the end of patterning, 1996 to 2005, as the happy years. With my dad back at work, she was the one most often at home with me and could watch, hour by hour, as I embraced my new life. She loved seeing how much I enjoyed sending email messages with my voice recognition system on my computer, connecting with new friends all over the country and eventually all over the world. She loved seeing my friends show up at our house, load me and my chair into our specially equipped van, and take off for the latest restaurant or pub or concert. She loved what became a cherished ritual for us, long visits to the nearest Barnes & Noble bookstore.

I had always been a deeply curious person, continuously pestering my parents with questions when I was young. I had a very wide range of interests, everything from aviation, meteorology, beekeeping, and history to science and computers. I could finally indulge those many interests on my own, principally through my lifelong love of reading. Mom followed me up one aisle of the sprawling bookstore and down the next, pulling down any title that caught my eye. She would place it on my lap so I could read the back cover, or she held it open so I could read the first few pages. On every visit we typically spent hours that way and always left the store with a new stack of titles, everything from Thucydides, the historian of ancient Greece, to Isaac Asimov and Mark Twain.

Of course, reading was also a necessarily shared experience.

"We tried an automatic page turner, but that never worked very well," my mom remembered in an interview with Tim Madigan. "So we used a stand that we put in front of Kevin's chair. The book had to be clipped open to the stand on both sides so it wouldn't close. He'd call us when he finished a page, or if he had been calling us a lot, he might wait for us to come in and check. We would take the book off of the stand, turn the page, and put it back and clip it, until he had finished the next page. Then we'd do it again."

I read hundreds of thousands of pages that way over the years, hundreds of books, but my parents never seemed to feel put-upon.

"It was just such a joy to see him read and appreciate the things he was reading, really a joy," my mom said. "And he was so appreciative. Always please and thank you. I asked him once, 'Don't you ever get tired of saying please and thank you?' He said, 'No, because I'm grateful.'"

I joined a local fraternal group, Young Men for Arlington, and was elected to its board of directors. I volunteered at a local shelter for abused women, supervising the computer room for the children, and became a mentor for Big Brothers Big Sisters. I did part-time computer work and formed a business designing websites and promoting high-tech assistance for those living with physical limitations. I discovered I had a knack for trading stocks online and playing online poker.

For a while there, I was making good spending money playing poker. I remember the markets would close at three o'clock our time, and my poker tournaments would start about the same time. So I would spend the first part of my day trading stocks and the second part winning at cards.

And I was determined to hit the road, to explore the world. Just a few months after patterning ended, I announced to my parents that I planned to attend an online gaming convention in Milwaukee, accompanied only by my recently hired personal attendant, Sedgwich Washington.

It would be my first trip on my own, without being accompanied by friends or family. I was not at all intimidated, and I was very excited. The unknown has always excited and intrigued me. When I asked myself the question, "Can I do this?" my answer was always, "I don't know, but I'm damn sure going to try!" My parents gulped when they heard of my plans but quickly agreed to them, as I knew they would.

"I remember being a little apprehensive about it," my mom remembered. "But he was so brave about everything."

Traveling, of course, was no simple matter for a person in my situation. We arrived at the airport early so my dad could supervise the dismantling of my wheelchair. Then he and Sedgwich carried me to my seat on the plane. I was on my way! Sedgwich and I checked into a Hyatt next door to the Milwaukee Convention Center, and then I was off on my own. I had the phone numbers of my online gaming partners, so we made plans to get together and hang out. But I had just as much fun rolling into the convention center by myself, making my way through thousands of people, just looking at them and all the exhibits. There were moments when I felt so intoxicated by the freedom that I felt as if I could literally take off in my chair.

That was just the beginning. I'll never forget another milestone, my trip to Chicago a few years later. I met up with

Steve Lord, another of Dick Lord's sons, who lived in the city, meeting Steve and his wife for dinner on Navy Pier at a famous place called Bubba Gump Shrimp Company. But for the rest of a three-day visit, I explored Chicago on my own, rolling up and down Michigan Avenue, through Grant Park, down the Lakefront, in and out of neighborhood bars, and to the observation deck at the top of Sears Tower. I've always been pretty ballsy and independent minded, and if I wanted to do something, I was going to find a way to do it or try very hard to find a way to do it. That trip to Chicago was certainly a different world from the one I had been living in for nearly fifteen years.

In the years after patterning, I did my best to make sure there was always another trip to look forward to. To Disney World in Orlando, to the Queen Mary and movie studios in Los Angeles, to the Alamo and River Walk in San Antonio, to the mountain resorts of Colorado.

And to the gaming tables of Las Vegas. On a warm summer afternoon in the late 1990s, I remember how the three of us roared down the Vegas strip in a rented red Mustang convertible. Greg Ticknor was behind the wheel. I sat next to him in the passenger seat. My brother, Kelly, rode in the back seat, with my chair crammed into the seat next to him.

My friendship with Greg had begun years before, in 1984, when he and Kelly were freshmen at the University of Texas–Arlington. They hit it off immediately, becoming fraternity brothers and roommates. Greg learned early on about the horror of that Sunday in 1981 and how it had turned our family's life upside down.

"Kelly was going to the ends of the earth, anything he could do to help Kevin physically, emotionally, and spiritually," Greg remembered decades later in an interview with Tim Madigan. "Kelly was a big cheerleader for Kev in those years."

Not long after Greg and Kelly met, my parents invited Greg to move in with us so he could save on rent money. Greg was grateful but was also amazed by what took place day after day in my garage apartment. He was never officially part of a patterning team, but Greg filled in whenever needed and supported our family however he could.

"It was extraordinary in so many ways—certainly for Kevin but for the entire family," Greg remembered. "The entire family's focal point was rallying around Kevin and patterning, because anybody and everybody was determined that this young man was going to get up and stand on his own two feet and walk on his own. That was the rallying cry for many years."

But Greg also saw firsthand the toll that patterning took on me and my family.

"It was physically exhausting, and I think emotionally it was a challenge too," Greg remembered. "Working that hard, that diligently, and doing it consistently day in and day out. Then, at the end of the week, when it was tallied up, and Kevin had moved eleven inches, that was somewhat disheartening.

"Kevin never really verbalized his frustration, but it was written on his face. I'm so proud of him. He maintained a positive attitude throughout this process. But at eight thirty at night, when it was time to shut the lights off, Kevin was just exhausted physically and emotionally."

Greg eventually found another place to live but remained close to Kelly and our family. In 1996 he was one of the first people Kelly called when I decided to stop patterning.

"It was a tough decision for Kelly to accept," Greg remembered. "It was a rock and a hard place. We wanted him to continue in the hopes that his limitations would decrease. But eventually you realize that he might have reached his physical limits. It was a tough pill to swallow. Kevin was eternally optimistic, but I think he was wrestling with the frustration. I think we all did. Reality has its place."

It was then, after patterning, that Kelly and Greg took on new roles in my life: trusted sidekicks. They were determined to help me explore aspects of life that had been denied to me for so long.

"It was a pleasure, but by the same token, it was a duty for a couple of guys like us," Greg recalled. "Kevin had a desire to travel a little bit, and shame on us if we didn't make that happen."

So the three of us roared into Las Vegas on that day in the late 1990s. I remember beaming in the passenger seat of the Mustang convertible, intoxicated by the lights, the noise, the crowds, the music, the life and energy of Vegas. We pulled into the famous Mirage hotel and checked in, and I insisted we immediately cross the strip to the Flamingo.

As it turned out, I was prepared. I like to research something before I do it. I don't like to be surprised, so before we left for Vegas, I learned that craps and blackjack had the best odds. I downloaded craps and blackjack games off the internet so I could practice, and I even learned something about counting cards. So we sidled up to the first craps table we came to and exchanged our cash for casino chips. I called out my bets. Greg and Kelly took turns rolling the dice. I remember blowing on them a time or two for luck. It seemed to work. The dice kept coming up in my favor. In terms of gambling, that sealed the deal. We moved to a blackjack table so I could try my hand at the game for real. Kelly and Greg pushed my chips forward, according to my instructions. It seemed the red-haired guy in the wheelchair created quite a stir. It was like something out of a movie.

"If I remember correctly, the pit boss thought he was counting cards," Greg remembered. "He was giving Kevin the look for quite a while because he was taking all their money. He was outsmarting the dealer. Kevin was hot. Kelly and I were hooting and hollering every time Kevin would win big. We determined right then who was buying dinner and drinks that night."

Between long stints at the tables, the three of us took in a performance by Siegfried and Roy, the legendary magicians and tiger trainers. I'll never forget the moment when one of the famous entertainers turned up out of the dark just a few feet from our table. That was thrilling.

"We had a fabulous time. Kevin didn't want it to end," Greg said. "I was just watching Kevin have the time of his life. If anybody deserved it . . . It's inspirational in so many ways for a guy who had been through what he had to figure out a way to call the glass half full. It was a monumental task, but he did it."

It seemed to my parents that they were meeting a new friend of mine every week, men and women who would show up at our house, introduce themselves, and then load me into the van and head to our local haunt, J. Gilligan's Irish pub in Arlington, or my favorite seafood place in Fort Worth, or to concerts by the Eagles or Willie Nelson.

My social media pages came to feature photograph after photograph of me, the lanky man in the wheelchair, typically in a long red beard, often wearing a playful hat, grinning broadly at the camera, surrounded by other beaming faces. Many of those faces belonged to beautiful women.

"I don't know how he did it," Greg Ticknor remembered, laughing.

It became second nature for my friends to lift a straw to my lips for a sip of a margarita, second nature to cut up my crab cakes, chicken-fried steak, or fried chicken and fork pieces into my mouth.

"I've never done this before," a new friend would say. "Do you want to ask for a drink before I help you?"

"I'll let you know," I would say.

"How can I help you eat?"

"Simple. Just cut up the food, put a bite on a fork, and instead of putting it in your piehole, put it in mine," I would say, with my trademark impish grin.

New acquaintances were, of course, curious about my disability.

"How long have you been in that chair?" a person would ask.

"About eight hours," I liked to reply, looking down at my watch, ever the wise guy.

Then I would share the story I had told hundreds of times before, but I never hesitated to tell it again, because I knew the curiosity was natural. Time had also worn away the sharpest edges of the trauma, so it was easy to offer a bare-bones recitation of the terrible facts.

"I was thirteen, in the eighth grade," I would begin. "My buddy and I were riding motorbikes on his property. We didn't know about it, but there was a neighbor who was apparently crazy, who thought we were making too much noise and came out with a shotgun and killed my friend, Trey, first, and then shot me in the head."

Nearby conversations in the bar or around the restaurant table tended to stop. I often saw tears in the eyes of my friends as I described what happened, and how the man named Richard Tiedemann had been shot and killed by the police.

"I'm glad the bastard is dead," was a typical response.

Friends lined up to embrace me when I finished the story. I often found myself comforting them.

"I went home and couldn't stop thinking about what you told us, and I couldn't stop crying," I often heard, or something to that effect.

But then it was back to the party, the laughter, the fun, because 1981 had been a long time ago. Patterning was finished. School was out. I was free, or so I thought.

René Cowart and her husband, Chris, were friends of my brother and his wife, and that night the couples ended up at the same table at an Arlington charity event. I was there as well and was introduced around. René was intrigued as she watched Kelly patiently cut up my food and fork it into my mouth and lift my margarita so I could take a sip through the straw, natural as can be.

René was also curious about the fact that I seemed reasonably happy and content, a disposition that seemed to belie my difficult circumstances. She said later she also found my whip-smart sense of humor to be endearing. Soon after we were introduced, I fired off a snarky remark, and René, as was her habit, fired one back. After the dinner, as Kelly, Mary Tom, and René's husband mingled with others, she and I snuck out to a quiet bar near the banquet room and ordered drinks.

"Excuse me," I said, smiling at her, nodding toward my waiting cocktail.

She laughed and did what she saw Kelly do—picked up my glass and put the straw to my lips. She asked the obvious question a few sips into our drinks.

"What happened to you?"

I think she expected to hear about an illness or an accident. The blood drained from René's face when I told her. She found it hard to believe my positive attitude could survive something so horrible. To her, I didn't seem to have an angry bone in my body or a care in the world.

"When he told me what happened, it shocked me, truly, but how he handled it shocked me even more," René said in an interview with Tim Madigan. "He was so happy and upbeat and full of life. I probably would have been in a hole somewhere. It's crazy to say this. I fell in love with him that night as someone who was one of my dearest and closest friends that I could trust with anything, because he's just that kind of guy. We talked about personal things that night. I'm not real open. I don't talk about personal things. But he and I talked about everything."

René became one of the most frequent visitors to our home, driving over with her two young children to load me up in the van and take me to a restaurant or back to her house for lunch.

"I would either cook something or pick something up," René remembered. "It was always about food. He likes to eat, and I like to eat. He likes to drink, and I like to drink. I would take a bite, then I would give him one. He would tell me when he wanted me to salt and pepper his food. He likes too much salt, and I would say, 'Kevin, lay off this shit.' And did you know he hates vegetables? He hates anything green."

Lunches often turned into dinners with René's family.

"He's so special to us," René said. "When our kids were growing up, they knew if he would be here for the Super Bowl or whatever, the kids knew to give him a drink, feed him some chips. They had a special bond with Kevin. He just loved kids. He would have been a great dad. A great husband."

Seeing me with her family gave René a special insight into what few others understood: how painful it was for me to think I would never be able to have a family of my own, and the degree to which I battled loneliness.

"Beneath the surface, I knew he was down on life," René said. "He wanted what everybody else had."

CHAPTER FOUR

The dream took hold early in the patterning years, when there was still hope that I might walk again: I wanted to be a fighter pilot, a pilot of any kind, really. I bought books on aviation, imagining myself at the controls of a cockpit, soaring through wide-open celestial spaces, untethered to the world of pain and limitation that was my reality on the ground. I learned about sailing too. I had dreams of sailing around the world solo, alone and on my own on the open ocean. I suppose it gets back to the same notion of crossing boundless frontiers, the freedom of that. Farming was another interest—raising cows and chickens and keeping bees—living off the land. Those were just a few of the several hundred things on my to-do list.

But as the patterning years passed and my progress continued to be measured in inches, I began to accept that my dreams were just that: dreams. It was not as if there was a sudden realization of that. The hope of walking again and doing of all those other things just slowly faded away. Gradually I knew they would not happen for me. I would have to reevaluate.

So I let go of the idea of flying, let go of farming, let go of the fantasy that someday I would be alone on the open seas. But one dream, one desire, would never really go away. I wanted to fall in love, marry, and have a family.

By that horrible winter day in 1981, girls had become a preoccupation with me, as they were for most boys my age. I was infatuated with this young lady or that one but always too shy to say so and had yet to be kissed. Then came Richard Tiedemann's ambush, the coma, and all those years of trying so desperately to get back on my feet. Through all of that, some might have assumed the shotgun pellet, which had taken away so much, had also erased my boyish desires. Though I never spoke of it to others, that certainly was not the case.

I still had my biology and those ancient male urges. After I was shot, I still thought about that, about having a girlfriend, but I kept those thoughts to myself. I'm a very private person and have never been the type to pour out my feelings to other people. When you combine that with the fact no one could do anything about my situation, there just didn't seem to be any need to talk about it. I suppose it was a blessing of sorts that the physical and emotional demands of patterning left little time or energy for loneliness. I was too exhausted most of the time. But after I stopped patterning, that would change.

Strange as it may seem, I became the envy of many men, because wherever I went in those days after patterning—to bars, restaurants, and the backyard barbecues where we gathered—beautiful women seemed to follow. Women seemed disproportionately intrigued by me. I still do not know exactly why. I don't consider myself particularly good-looking. And I don't consider myself particularly charming. Maybe it's the fact I always tried to be kind and happy. Maybe it's because I have such a terrible personal story but always try to have a loving and pleasant disposition. Whatever the reason or reasons, I realize how lucky and blessed I am.

"When I would see him in a social setting, whether it would be at J. Gilligan's pub or wherever, these women would be doting on Kevin," Greg Ticknor remembered. "They would want to hug on him, love on him, talk to him, help him with his meals and his drinks. I think Kevin certainly had the desire to take some of those relationships to the next level, but I don't think that was ever the desire of the woman."

What people did not know was how I fought a constant inner battle. There was sexual desire, hopes to find a partner, get married, and have a family. There was my inherent shyness around the opposite sex that had afflicted me since boyhood. Then there was the reality of my limited circumstances. Occasionally, I put out subtle cues to a woman, indicating my desire to take a friendship to a different place. I was always gently rebuffed. When that happened over and over again, I figured it just wasn't in the cards for me. I was very sad about it. I was also very angry about it, but not angry at the women. I was angry about the situation. From a woman's perspective, I totally understood. It was too much to ask of another person. They would have to be a caregiver as well as a companion. I could already see it was a huge burden on my friends and family. They did it out of love, of course, and wouldn't have had it any other way. But in terms of a life partner, eventually I decided I couldn't ask someone or even allow someone to take on that burden.

So I tried to become resigned to the loneliness I assumed would always be a part of my life. I loved those nights out with friends, the laughter and the music. I was always the one who wanted to stay out until last call. But one of the reasons for that, I now realize, is that I hated the idea that I would return to an empty apartment, that I would always go home alone. Friends would drop me off, and I would let myself in through my self-opening electric door. I would recline in my chair and try to sleep because I didn't want to wake my parents. But before dozing off, I often stared into the darkness, sometimes for hours, the reality of my loneliness covering me like a thick, wet blanket. I thought about how different my life might have been had Trey and I not ridden into Richard Tiedemann's crosshairs.

I had a lot of friends and was certainly grateful for that. I was glad that people thought I was a good guy, witty, fun to be around, someone who cared about others. It was great to go out and have a good time. But when you always come home alone, during those nights in my room, it really didn't matter how charming and witty other people thought I was.

But the sun would come up on another day. There were books to read, emails to send, stocks to trade, poker hands to play, trips to plan and take, and before long another late-night frolic with friends. By any reasonable definition, I was happy, especially when compared to the excruciating and draining efforts of the years before. Bouts of intense loneliness came and went for years, but only intermittently.

Something shifted early in 2005. It happened so gradually that I scarcely noticed how the nights of loneliness became ever more frequent, or how my despair became even more intense. I was powerless to banish the dark thoughts that swirled through my head in the seemingly endless hours of the night and kept me from sleep. I was haunted more and more by the litany of all of the things I would never be able to do, a list that played on an endless loop in my brain. I would never fly a plane; I would never sail a ship at sea; I would never fall in love with a woman who was in love with me; I would never get married; I would never be a father.

Never. That was the thing. It got to a point where it wasn't just episodes of loneliness. It was a constant and infinite loneliness. I couldn't see a point where it ended, other than with my death. It was a cumulative thing, building up day after day, month after month, year after year, a slow drip, drip, drip, like Chinese water torture. Anyone can suffer pretty much anything if it's for a finite time, especially if they can say to themselves, "Well, this will be over tomorrow or next week, or even next year." But my situation was permanent. I would be suffering like this for fifty or sixty years, until I died. I could look years and years ahead, and as far as I could see into the future, I could see only more loneliness and more pain, and the more I thought about it and the more I dwelled upon it, the more infinite the suffering seemed to be.

Richard Tiedemann also began to increasingly infiltrate my thoughts. Over the years I had occasionally seen the madman's grainy photograph in old newspapers, but otherwise I had no clue about the man who shot Trey and me. Tiedemann became an amorphous monster waiting in the trees with his shotgun, intent on killing Trey and me for no good reason. It wasn't a car accident. The fact this guy intentionally set out to murder both of us . . . that left me with a gnawing anger and a total incomprehension of his motives. What was he thinking? Why would he do this to us, but especially to me, because I was the one left to suffer, paralyzed forever? My inability to understand Tiedemann's motives troubled me for a long time. Not that I wanted vengeance. He was already dead. I just desperately wanted to understand. It was all so bizarre. I've since learned there is no rational explanation for an irrational act, but back then I was just so hurt and angry and confused.

It wasn't long before I began to dread the dark. The nighttime was when the demons came to torment me. More and more I felt trapped in a lifeless body, and I came to believe my mind existed only to torture me. It felt as if a vise were slowly tightening upon my head, slowly but inexorably crushing my mind and my soul and my spirit. And there was nothing I could do about it. Nothing at all. The pain would never go away. All I had to look forward to, for the rest of my life, was endless and excruciating pain.

My despair morphed into a deep depression that began to bleed into the daytime hours. Email messages from friends went unreturned. I put on movies to pass the time, but afterward I couldn't remember what they had been about. A book sat open to the same page day after day. I found myself turning down most social invitations because it took too much energy to pretend to be the same happy, caring, witty Kevin.

If my friends noticed, no one said so. The one person who

did notice was my mom. She would ask me if there was something wrong. I would tell her that I was just tired or preoccupied or busy. Otherwise, I never spoke to anyone about how I was feeling. What was the point? This was my problem, and talking about it wasn't going to erase my physical limitations. Talking about it wouldn't change anything, so I would just sit in my chair and lean back and think about how bad it was and how miserable I was.

Eventually, I came to see only one way out. I became more and more preoccupied with taking my life, but even those thoughts were frustrating. How could I kill myself if I couldn't pick up a gun or open a bottle of pills? So, even in this regard, my means were very limited, to say the least. I thought about just rolling out in front of a bus, but I didn't want to put someone in the position of running over me and then having to live with that.

I finally settled on a plan. I would get a ride to nearby Lake Arlington on the pretense that I wanted to spend a few hours alone looking at the water. I would then roll down the dock in my motorized wheelchair when no one was looking and plunge off the end into the water. Finally, my suffering would be over. I would do it one day soon. Maybe tomorrow. Maybe the next day. Maybe next week.

I realize now that the inborn desire to live was still pretty strong in me. I think that's what kept me from acting sooner. I was also hesitant to do that to my family and friends. They would not understand. But my pain was getting worse and worse, and it got to a point where I could see no hope at all.

The only thing I had to look forward to, I thought, was endless pain and endless suffering. The pain of my loved ones would eventually be superseded by my own. It was only a matter of time before I took my own life. Not only did I feel that way; I was sure of it.

CHAPTER FIVE

The hundreds of books that filled the shelves of my apartment were arranged so that I could read the titles from my wheelchair. That's what I was doing on that day in the late summer of 2005—searching my library for something that might distract me from my gloom.

Basic Physics.

The Archeology of Mesopotamia.

The Lord of the Rings, by J. R. R. Tolkien.

The Collected Works of Jack London.

Black Belt in Blackjack.

Exodus, by Leon Uris.

A Practical Guide for the Beginning Farmer.

Nothing really grabbed me. I was about to give up, tilt back in my chair, and resume staring at the ceiling or out of the window, when a book finally caught my attention. Several years before, I had purchased a copy of *The 7 Habits of Highly Effective People: Powerful Lessons in Personal Change*. Ralph Shelton and my brother, Kelly, both swore by Stephen Covey's book, which was a monster bestseller, particularly popular among business types. But until that fateful day in 2005, it had been gathering dust on my bookshelf. Looking back on that time so long ago, I can only think how very fortunate I was to finally decide to read that book. Call it luck, call it happenstance, or call it a wondrous miracle, but it happened, and my life was forever changed because of it.

Not that I was consciously looking for "personal change," as Covey's subtitle implied. Instead, there were more prosaic and practical reasons for my interest. For all my despair, I had not completely given up hope of getting ahead in the world and making money. Based on the book's popularity, I assumed Covey would provide some helpful tips to that end.

That, more than anything, was why I asked my mother to take *The 7 Habits* down from its place on my bookshelf. She pinned it open on the first page and then left the room. With that simple act, I began a journey of healing that would save my life and eventually introduce me to the wisdom of the ages. I read the first two paragraphs:

"In more than twenty-five years of working with people in business, university, and marriage and family settings, I have come in contact with many individuals who have achieved an incredible degree of outward success, but have found themselves struggling with an inner hunger, a deep need for personal congruency and effectiveness and for healthy, growing relationships with other people," Covey wrote.

"These are deep problems, painful problems—problems that quick-fix approaches can't solve."*

I got no further on that first day, because something in what I had read stopped me cold. *Deep problems, painful problems. No quick fixes*. I reread the first two paragraphs, deeply moved and intrigued. Why would a popular business book start out with a description of the nature of human suffering? Yet something had stirred inside me, a fluttering I would later recognize as the beginnings of hope. The first paragraphs of Covey's book seemed to imply that it would suggest a path forward through the inevitable pain of life. And not only a path forward; it seemed to say there was a bridge over this unfathomable river of pain and despair I was feeling. I needed that so much more than tips on how to make money. If only I could find the way . . .

I lingered over every sentence when I resumed reading. It was early on, on page 8, that I came across one of Covey's foundational theories: humans see the world through their own distorted prisms, and their lenses are often clouded by their individual personalities, histories, and circumstances. Yet often those perceptions have very little to do with reality. What was needed, Covey suggested, was a new way of seeing things.

---

* From THE 7 HABITS OF HIGHLY EFFECTIVE PEOPLE by Stephen R. Covey.

"We must look at the lens through which we see the world, as well as at the world we see. . .The lens itself shapes how we interpret the world."

It's no exaggeration to say that with those few words, I felt as if the foundation of my life had been snatched out from beneath me. Since the day Trey and I had been shot, I had looked at the world through the lens of tragedy and suffering, a perspective that was as much a part of me as my very limbs—and a misery to which I felt entitled. It had never even occurred to me that there was any way of looking at my life other than what had happened to me was horrible, and that my life was horrible as a result. I couldn't see through any other lens. That was set in concrete. And then, all of a sudden, I found out I might be totally wrong about the way I saw the world and the way I saw myself in it. The feeling was very disorienting and unsettling, to say the least.

The book sat open to that same page for days as I turned Covey's words over and over in my mind. As I examined this new concept and tried to look at it from all angles, I found that just doing this was very healing. I was surprised to realize that the author's vaguely spiritual notions had shouldered aside my constant preoccupation with my own suffering. Entire days passed without a thought of suicide. The vise on my head seemed to be loosening. It was like being in a burning building where you can't see anything, and you don't know how to get out. You can't see any doors or windows. And then, through the smoke and flames, you see a window, and you know there might be a way out. You're not out yet. You're still in mortal danger. You're still inside a burning building. But you can see a window, and you realize there could be a way out after all. I now thought I could see that window, a way out of my pain and torment.

The irony, as I reflect upon it many years later, is that until my chance encounter with *The 7 Habits*, I had almost no interest in spirituality, and even less in the self-help remedies and pop psychology proliferating in the culture at that time. I had been taught the virtues of integrity, compassion, kindness, and perseverance by my parents, who had modeled them day after day from the time I was old enough to remember, but particularly after I was shot and through the long patterning years. Their example was the source of my best character traits, not the dogma of the Christian church in which I was nominally raised. I was in the pew with my family on Sundays, and I belonged to church youth groups, but church was more of a social thing than anything spiritual. In truth, God was mostly irrelevant to my young life, and to the extent I thought about religion at all, it didn't make much sense to me.

I had always equated spirituality with religion, but I found out much later that one has little to do with the other. And talk of a higher power, or "God," for lack of a better word, seemed totally make-believe to me. I just couldn't buy into anything that I couldn't see and couldn't hear and wasn't of this world. It wasn't like I was a hard disbeliever or an atheist. It just didn't mean anything to me.

Also, when I was growing up, I knew there were a lot of Christian people who said *their* religion was the only way to live and to go to heaven. But billions of other people of other religions argued that *their* way was the only way to live and the only way to know God. I kind of just threw up my hands.

It's true that after I was shot, patterning became a religion of sorts. My salvation would come not through faith or prayer, but in day after day of agonizing struggle. Nor did I experience a spiritual awakening in the years after my rehab program ended. Then, even when my despair became life-threatening, never for a second did I consider seeking professional help or the possibility that relief could be found in the pages of a book. I could talk to a therapist or a psychologist until I was blue in the face, but I would still be in my situation. I would always be a quadriplegic. That's why I never even bothered.

On the surface, Stephen Covey's seven habits were easy enough to dismiss as business-school-sounding mumbo jumbo.

Habit 1: Be proactive.

Habit 2: Begin with the end in mind.

Habit 3: Put first things first.

Habit 4: Think win-win.

Habit 5: Seek first to understand, then to be understood.

Habit 6: Synergize.

Habit 7: Sharpen the saw. (Whatever that meant.)

Covey's theories turned out to be anything but simplistic, based instead on the author's decades of study of human behavior. The Mormon businessman, educator, and counselor used the seven habits as the framework for a profound analysis of the human condition. In the last century, Covey wrote, Western culture seemed to have strayed from the foundational human virtues upon which truly meaningful lives were based. Covey called them the "Character Ethic . . . things like integrity, humility, fidelity, temperance, courage, justice, patience, industry, simplicity, modesty and the Golden Rule." He went on:

> The reality of such principles or natural laws becomes obvious to anyone who thinks deeply and examines the cycles of social history. These principles surface time and time again, and the degree to which people in a society recognize and live in harmony with them moves them toward either survival and stability or disintegration and destruction.
>
> The principles I am referring to are not esoteric, mysterious, or "religious" ideas. There is not one principle taught in this book that is unique to any specific faith or religion, including my own. These principles are a part of most every major enduring religion, as well as enduring social philosophies and ethical systems. They are self-evident and can easily be validated by any individual. It's almost as if these principles or natural laws are part of the human condition, part of the human consciousness, part of the human conscience. They seem to exist in all human beings, regardless of social conditioning and loyalty to them, even though they might be submerged or numbed by such conditions or disloyalty.

I immediately recognized Covey's virtues. In reading about them, I was reminded of how deeply they were ingrained in my own being, and how fundamental they were to my sense of myself. Covey's words about humility and courage and kindness always meant a great deal to me, and they still do. Again, that was one of the precious gifts from my parents.

I was also intrigued by how Covey's theories contradicted the conventional wisdom about how to get ahead in life—that personal ambition was the root of success and material possessions its measure. Covey argued instead that success could only be achieved through the cultivation of inner virtue. This very much resonated with what I felt was deep inside of me.

> We need a new level, a deeper level of thinking—a paradigm based on the principles that accurately describe the territory of effective human being and interacting—to solve these deep concerns.
>
> This new level of thinking is what *The 7 Habits of Highly Effective People* is about. It's a principle-centered, character-based, "inside-out" approach to personal and interpersonal effectiveness. "Inside-out" means to start first with self; even more fundamentally, to start with the most inside part of self—with your paradigms, your character, and your motives.
>
> It says if you want to have a happy marriage, be the kind of person who generates positive energy and sidesteps negative energy rather than empowering it. If you want to have a more pleasant, cooperative teenager, be a more

> understanding, empathic, consistent, loving parent. If you want to have more freedom, more latitude in your job, be a more responsible, a more helpful, a more contributing employee. If you want to be trusted, be trustworthy. If you want the secondary greatness of recognized talent, focus first on primary greatness of character.
>
> The inside-out approach says that private victories precede public victories, that making and keeping promises to ourselves precedes making and keeping promises to others. It says it is futile to put personality ahead of character, to try to improve relationships with others before improving ourselves. Inside-out is a process—a continuing process of renewal based on the natural laws that govern human growth and progress. It's an upward spiral of growth that leads to progressively higher forms of responsible independence and effective interdependence.
>
> I have had the opportunity to work with many people—wonderful people, talented people, people who deeply want to achieve happiness and success, people who are searching, people who are hurting. I've worked with business executives, college students, church and civic groups, families and marriage partners. And in all of my experience, I have never seen lasting solutions to problems, lasting happiness and success that came from the outside in.

On many days during this period, when my mom would come in to turn the page in my book, she found me not reading but staring off into the day. I had done that a lot when my despair was deepest, but I think my mom sensed that there was something different about this reverie.

"Just thinking," I would tell her, smiling.

I came across Covey's strange exercise about fifty pages into *The 7 Habits:*

> As you read this book, try to stand apart from yourself. Try to project your consciousness upward into a corner of the room and see yourself, in your mind's eye, reading. Can you look at yourself almost as though you were someone else?
>
> Now try something else. Think about the mood you are now in. Can you identify it? What are you feeling? How would you describe your present mental state?
>
> Your ability to do what you just did is uniquely human. Animals do not possess this ability. We call it "self-awareness" or the ability to think about your very thought process. This is the reason why man has dominion over all things in the world and why he can make significant advances from generation to generation. This is why we can evaluate and learn from others' experiences as well as our own. This is also why we can make and break our habits.
>
> We are not our feelings. We are not our moods. We are not even our thoughts. The very fact that we can think about these things separates us from them and from the animal world. Self-awareness enables us to stand apart and examine

> even the way we "see" ourselves—our self-paradigm, the most fundamental paradigm of effectiveness. It affects not only our attitudes and behaviors, but also how we see other people. It becomes our map of the basic nature of mankind.

I decided to give it a try. I imagined myself in a corner of my apartment, looking at the man in the wheelchair, peering into that man's mind and heart as a third party would, a neutral observer. As I did, I was surprised by the compassion I felt for that person in the wheelchair and was amazed to think about all that he had gone through. For the first time, I also began to see myself as other people saw me. I was okay after all. It made sense that other people loved and respected me.

Finally, through this strange exercise, looking down at this man, I realized the extent to which I had become a prisoner of my own thoughts of despair, and how those chaotic thoughts were contributing to my agony. That was so important. I realized I was not my feelings or my emotions or even my thoughts. I could stand apart from them, and with that distance, I could examine them, really examine them, for the first time. I didn't have to automatically react with anger or sadness or desperation to these things swirling around inside my head. Instead, I could rip them apart, deconstruct these thoughts, and try to dig down to the truth. By standing apart from my feelings, I could see them from the outside in.

But Covey took it one step further. Not only did humans have the capacity to stand apart from their thoughts and to observe them dispassionately, but each person had the freedom to choose how to react to those feelings. The author quoted Gandhi: "They cannot take away our self-respect if we do not give it to them." Covey explained, "It is our willing permission, our consent to what happens to us, that hurts us far more than what happens to us in the first place. I admit this is very hard to accept emotionally, especially if we have had years and years of explaining our misery in the name of circumstance or someone else's behavior. But until a person can say deeply and honestly, 'I am what I am today because of the choices I made yesterday,' that person cannot say, 'I choose otherwise.'"

In his book, Covey told the story of a woman in the audience at one of his lectures, a nurse who was required to care for a difficult patient, day after day:

> "This man has made my life miserable, and I often take my frustration out on my family. The other nurses feel the same way. We almost pray for his demise," she told Covey after the lecture. "And for you to have the gall to stand up there and suggest that nothing can hurt me, that no one can hurt me without my consent, and that I have chosen my own emotional life of being miserable—well, there was just no way I could buy into that.
>
> "But I kept thinking about it. I really went inside myself and began to ask, 'Do I have the power to choose my response?' When I finally realized that I do have that power, when I swallowed that bitter pill and realized that I had chosen to be miserable, I also realized that I could choose not to be miserable.

> "At that moment I stood up. I felt as though I was being let out of San Quentin. I wanted to yell to the whole world, 'I am free! I am let out of prison! No longer am I going to be controlled by the treatment of some person.'"

But I have to admit, for me that finally seemed a bridge too far. Covey's theory might be fine for a nurse with a difficult patient or a person with a disagreeable spouse or a parent with an unruly child or an employee with an overbearing boss. But my suffering was of a completely different order. I was paralyzed and alone forever because of an evil act of a madman. What other way was there to look at *that*? It wasn't so much a criticism of Covey as it was a recognition that my situation was so horrible. I didn't think it was at all comparable to what Covey was writing about. I had serious doubts as to whether any of this could be helpful to me.

But then Covey introduced me to Viktor Frankl, an Austrian Jew and, prior to World War II, a prominent young psychiatrist:

> He was imprisoned in the death camps of Nazi Germany, where he experienced things that were so repugnant to our sense of decency that we shudder to even repeat them. His parents, his brother, and his wife died in the camps or were sent to the gas ovens. Except for his sister, his entire family perished. Frankl himself suffered torture and innumerable indignities, never knowing from one moment to the next if his path would lead to the ovens or if he would be among the "saved" who would remove the bodies or shovel out the

ashes of those so fated. One day, naked and alone in a small room, he began to become aware of what he later called "the last of the human freedoms"—the freedom his Nazi captors could not take away.

CHAPTER SIX

There was an unusual urgency in my request to my mother on that autumn day in 2005. I needed to get to Barnes & Noble to find a book called *Man's Search for Meaning*, Viktor Frankl's twentieth-century masterpiece of philosophy and psychology. But then my mom reminded me that I already owned a copy. It had been a gift during the patterning years from my friend and mentor Dick Lord. She quickly found it on my bookshelf, and I read the pastor's inscription.

"I hope this book means as much to you as it did to me," Lord had written.

By the time of Frankl's death in 1997, *Man's Search for Meaning* had been translated into twenty-four languages and sold more than twelve million copies. From its first pages, however, I felt the author was writing to me alone, challenging my skepticism in ways which were inarguable.

I had felt doomed to a life of despair and loneliness because of the evil that had befallen me, but in *Man's Search for Meaning*, I discovered someone whose acquaintance with horror, anguish, and injustice had been every bit as acute as my own. Not only had Frankl survived the Holocaust; he had somehow managed to transcend his suffering and share his experience for the benefit of a broken world.

"I do not at all see in the bestseller status of my book an achievement and accomplishment on my part but rather an expression of the misery of our time," Frankl wrote in the preface to his book. "If hundreds of thousands of people reach out for a book whose very title promises to deal with the question of a meaning to life, it must be a question that burns under their fingernails . . . I had wanted simply to convey to the reader by way of a concrete example that life holds a potential meaning under any conditions, even the most miserable ones. And I thought that if the point was demonstrated in a situation as extreme as that in a concentration camp, my book might gain a hearing. I therefore felt responsible for writing down what I had gone through, for I thought it might be helpful to people who are prone to despair."*

More than any of the many works of philosophy and spirituality that I would devour in the years to come, *Man's Search for Meaning* transformed my life. I thought I had been condemned to a meaningless existence, growing old alone in my wheelchair, unable to contribute anything, dependent on others until my last breath, but here was a man whose suffering I couldn't dismiss. If Viktor Frankl could find meaning in the Holocaust, I could find meaning in what had happened to me. Or at least I could try.

---

* From MAN'S SEARCH FOR MEANING by Viktor Frankl. Copyright © 1959, 1962, 1984, 1992 by Viktor Frankl. Reprinted with permission from Beacon Press, Boston, Massachusetts.

"Then the train shunted, obviously nearing a main station. Suddenly a cry broke from the ranks of the anxious passengers, 'There is a sign, Auschwitz!' Everyone's heart missed a beat at that moment. Auschwitz—the very name stood for all that was horrible: gas chambers, crematoriums, massacres. Slowly, almost hesitatingly, the train moved on as if it wanted to spare its passengers the dreadful realization as long as possible: Auschwitz!"

In the years before his arrival at one of the Nazis' most notorious death camps, Viktor Frankl had been one of the most respected young psychiatrists in Austria, a protégé of Sigmund Freud. As the Nazi menace grew, Frankl turned down an opportunity to flee and continue his work in the United States, choosing instead to stay in Austria in order to try to protect his elderly parents. He and his family were rounded up in 1942, and almost all of them perished in the Holocaust. Frankl himself was reduced to a number—119104—and ordered into slave labor to lay railroad lines or dig tunnels and otherwise join "the hard fight for existence which raged among the prisoners. This was an unrelenting struggle for daily bread and for life itself."

The first sixty pages of *Man's Search for Meaning* are a grim and unstinting depiction of that struggle.

> The thought of suicide was entertained by nearly everyone, if only for a brief time. It was born of the hopelessness of the situation, the constant danger of death looming over us daily and hourly, and the closeness of the deaths suffered by many of the others. From personal convictions which will

be mentioned later, I made myself a firm promise, on my first evening in camp, that I would not "run into the wire." This was a phrase used in camp to describe the most popular method of suicide—touching the electrically charged barbed-wire fence. It was not entirely difficult for me to make this decision. There was little point in committing suicide, since, for the average inmate, life expectation, calculating objectively and counting all likely chances, was very poor. He could not with any assurance expect to be among the small percentage of men who survived all the selections. The prisoner of Auschwitz, in the first phase of shock, did not fear death. Even the gas chambers lost their horrors for him after the first few days—after all, they spared him the act of committing suicide . . .

But the prisoner who had passed into the second stage of his psychological reactions did not avert his eyes anymore. By then his feelings were blunted, and he watched unmoved. Another example: he found himself waiting at sick bay, hoping to be granted two days of light work inside the camp because of injuries or perhaps edema or fever. He stood unmoved while a twelve-year-old boy was carried in who had been forced to stand at attention for hours in the snow or to work outside with bare feet because there were no shoes for him in the camp. His toes had become frostbitten, and the doctor on duty picked off the black gangrenous stumps with tweezers, one by one. Disgust, horror and pity are emotions that our spectator could not really feel any more. The sufferers, the dying and the dead, became such

> commonplace sights to him after a few weeks of camp life that they could not move him anymore.

As horrible as they were, such portrayals of Nazi death camps became commonplace in world literature in the decades after World War II, as did stories of Holocaust liberation and survival, such as Frankl's. But he had a broader point to make in the book that poured out of him in nine days in 1946. *A Psychologist Experiences the Concentration Camp* was published that year. It was renamed *Man's Search for Meaning* when it came out in the United States in 1959.

The book landed with the force of revelation because of the questions it posed and attempted to answer:

> Does man have no choice of action in the face of such circumstances? We can answer these questions from experience as well as on principle. The experiences of camp life show that man does have a choice of action. There were enough examples, often of a heroic nature, which proved that apathy could be overcome, irritability suppressed. Man can preserve a vestige of spiritual freedom, of independence of mind, even in such terrible conditions of psychic and physical stress.
>
> We who lived in concentration camps can remember the men who walked through the huts comforting others, giving away their last piece of bread. They may have been few in number, but they offer sufficient proof that everything can be taken from a man but one thing: the last of the human

> freedoms—to choose one's attitude in any given set of circumstances, to choose one's own way.
>
> And there were always choices to make. Every day, every hour, offered the opportunity to make a decision, a decision which determined whether you would or would not submit to those powers which threatened to rob you of your very self, your inner freedom; which determined whether or not you would become the plaything of circumstance.

If anyone had been a plaything of circumstance, it was me. And Trey had been as well. I had also read and heard about countless other people, good people forced to endure tragedy or terrible misfortune merely because they had been in the wrong place at the wrong time. No wonder so many shared my belief that the world was both random and cruel.

And yet there were a handful of people in the Nazi death camps, Viktor Frankl among them, who had refused to surrender their inner lives to the forces of evil and caprice, who had managed to cling to their "spiritual freedom." I was determined to find out exactly what that meant and to try to do the same thing, if I could possibly find the strength within myself to do so.

> Dostoyevsky said once, "There is only one thing that I dread: not to be worthy of my sufferings." These words frequently came to my mind after I became acquainted with those martyrs whose behavior in camp, whose suffering and death, bore witness to the fact that the last inner freedom cannot be lost. It can be said that they were worthy of their

> sufferings; the way they bore their suffering was a genuine inner achievement. It is this spiritual freedom—which cannot be taken away—that makes life meaningful and purposeful.
>
> The way in which a man accepts his fate and all the suffering it entails, the way in which he takes up his cross, gives him ample opportunity—even under the most difficult circumstances—to add a deeper meaning to his life. He may remain brave, dignified and unselfish. Or in the bitter fight for self-preservation he may forget his human dignity and become no more than an animal. Here lies the chance for a man either to make use of or to forgo the opportunities of attaining the moral values that a difficult situation may afford him. And this decides whether he is worthy of his sufferings or not.

Could I be worthy? Could I manage to find meaning in my life despite what had happened to me? For the first time since I stopped patterning, I felt as if I had a purpose. I took that quote from Dostoyevsky and the writings of Frankl as a direct challenge. Could I live to suffer bravely and heroically and with dignity? Or would I take the other path and wallow in self-pity and despair? I have always been up for a challenge. I can be a very stubborn person, and if I set my mind to something, I am going to achieve it, if it's at all possible. I launched myself into this challenge with the same will and determination that I used in patterning, but it was certainly a very different endeav-or. You could almost say patterning was superficial. It would have affected my outer being, my physical circumstances. But I felt that this was a much larger challenge than trying to learn how to walk again. It was potentially a much more rewarding challenge. I could transform my entire being. I could transform the way I looked at my life and the way I looked at life itself.

> What was really needed was a fundamental change in our attitude toward life. We had to learn ourselves and, furthermore, we had to teach the despairing man, that it did not really matter what we expected from life, but rather what life expected from us . . . No man and no destiny can be compared with any other man or any other destiny. No situation repeats itself, and each situation calls for a different response . . . Sometimes man may be required simply to accept fate, to bear his cross. Every situation is distinguished by its uniqueness and there is always only one right answer to the problem posed by the situation at hand.

To one degree or another, since the day I woke up in the hospital, I had believed that life had conspired against me. My hopes for happiness and fulfillment had been crushed by a mad gunman and a capricious universe. I certainly recognized myself as the despairing man to which Frankl referred, the man who needed to be taught. And I was finally willing. For the first time in my life, I started to ask myself a different question.

What did life expect from me?

The answer was immediately obvious. I had always known it, deep down. The answer to that question was to overcome my circumstances and to live in peace and harmony, with bravery and compassion and unconditional love for others, not only for the people I knew but also for those I didn't know. It wasn't spelled out in anything I had read. It was just something I felt. I knew it with an absolute certainty. My answer was simply the natural extension and progression of my life. Everything I had been through, and everything I had been raised to believe, was all leading to unconditional love for everyone, despite what had happened to me. The hard part was getting there.

In the fall and winter of 2005–2006, after finishing my first pass through the books of Covey and Frankl, I chose to sit in undistracted silence for hours each day. Drawing upon the ideas of those two writers, I consciously observed my thoughts and feelings, moment by moment. Through that process, I became much more aware of how ingrained the thoughts of loss and loneliness had become, and how quickly they could slip past my mental defenses to trigger old agonies. At first it was like a sordid game of Whac-A-Mole—this terrible thought, this painful feeling, then that one, then another. But then I realized something else. Just making the effort to observe my painful thoughts seemed to dilute their power, making it easier for me to try to substitute thoughts of peace and love for those negative thoughts. For example, a thought would cross my mind: "I'll never be a husband and a father," and then the anger would come, and the overwhelming sadness. But then I would recognize that it was just a thought. I could feel the associated feelings, but I also could consciously try to think another way. "I may never be a husband and a father, true, but nothing about that can stop me from fulfilling my purpose. I can live a life of courage and dignity no matter what my circumstances might be. I can be worthy of my suffering, and I can always love. Nothing can stop me from doing that."

I realized there was something very familiar in what I was attempting to do. I was trying to pattern my troubled mind and heart as I had once attempted to reprogram my broken body. That's what I was aiming for. I would go through this process over and over and over again during the course of a day, replacing thoughts of pain with thoughts of love. It wasn't that I was trying to kid myself or distract myself. I was consciously trying to build a foundation, a bedrock upon which to base my life.

I kept at it for days, and then weeks, and then months, and I slowly began to realize my spiritual patterning was succeeding where my physical patterning had failed. My spiritual journey was just beginning, but I sensed that my life had somehow been changed forever. It's not as if I had a goal for myself, an inner state of mind I wanted to achieve. Like they say, it's not the destination, it's the journey. Gradually I began to realize it was becoming easier and easier, almost second nature, to replace thoughts of pain with thoughts of love. The thoughts of pain eventually became the exception. The thoughts of love were now becoming the rule.

But they were no longer simply thoughts. Just months before, I had felt as if the vise on my head were being constantly tightened. Now I had the palpable sensation of inner freedom, of light spilling out from within me, a light that illuminated every situation in which I found myself and every person I encountered. The light did not distinguish between a rose petal and Richard Tiedemann.

Dick Lord, the pastor of Rush Creek Christian Church, had been preaching on that Super Bowl Sunday in 1981 when Trey and I had fidgeted in the pews, waiting to be released into a gorgeous winter day. A few hours later, after the shooting, Dick had tried to comfort the youth group at the church and then joined the vigil at the Arlington hospital where I clung to life. From that time on, though my family and I no longer attended church because of the patterning schedule, Dick remained a devoted friend to me, a mainstay throughout the patterning years, someone we could always count on. It was fitting that Dick had given me my copy of *Man's Search for Meaning*.

After patterning had ended, the pastor made it a point to stay in touch, visiting me a couple of times a year. In breezy and superficial conversations in my apartment, we reminisced about the days before the shooting, when I used to tag along after Kelly, Jimmy Lord, and other friends of theirs. I told Dick about my various business pursuits and the details of my very active social life. I had no interest then in the deeper questions of existence, much less in discussing them.

But that had changed by the spring of 2006. Months of reading and contemplation had delivered me into this strange and wondrous place, a mysterious new existence of peace and of light and of love. I half expected that my difficult life circumstances would eventually pull me back down into the pit of despair. But as the weeks and months passed, my inner joy lingered. Indeed, it grew stronger with the passage of time. By the spring of 2006, twenty-five years after I was shot, I called Dick and asked for a meeting at the church.

Sedgwich Washington, my attendant, drove me to Rush Creek on the appointed day. Dick greeted me warmly, curious to know what I was so eager to discuss. Then he listened as I, for the first time, confided to another person about the depths of my despair the previous year, and how close I had come to taking my own life. But that was not why I had come. I described my fateful encounter with Stephen Covey's book, the life-changing impact of Viktor Frankl, and a spiritual awakening that at times seemed almost overwhelming.

"I don't know exactly what this is or where it's coming from," I told Dick that day. "But I know one thing for certain: I've let go of all my hatred, all of my anger, and all of my sadness. What I have left in place of all of that is an overwhelming feeling of love and of peace in my heart. As I said, I don't really understand it, but I know it's real, the truest thing I have ever experienced."

Dick smiled and nodded. I saw that my friend's eyes were glistening.

"All those years we tried to heal your body," he said. "Maybe this is the healing you've been looking for all along."

"Yes, and I need to share this with others," I said. "I've learned so very much about love, and about happiness, and about finding peace within myself, and I feel a need to share this gift I've received. I don't know where to start, but I thought maybe you could help point me in the right direction."

Derek Tompkins had grown up in the Rush Creek congregation, and over the years he had heard the story of Super Bowl Sunday 1981 and the terrible events that had occurred just across the street from the church on Bowen Road. But until that quiet Wednesday morning of January 25, 2006, he and I had never met. It was the twenty-fifth anniversary of the shooting, and I wanted to place some flowers at the church in remembrance of Trey. Tompkins, Rush Creek's new youth minister, later said he was surprised to look out and see me rolling across the parking lot. Sedgwich walked with me, carrying the bouquet of flowers I had purchased earlier that morning. Derek greeted us outside, introducing himself.

"I know that this is the anniversary," he said. "I'm very sorry."

I thanked him.

"I didn't want the day to pass without doing something to remember and honor Trey," I said.

Derek suggested that a memorial garden outside the church might be a good place to reflect and to leave the flowers. He excused himself, and I asked Sedgwich to wait at the van so I could spend a few silent minutes there. Then Sedgwich and I drove off into the winter day.

I found out later that Derek thought I seemed tense and somber that day, which was not surprising under the circumstances. But the young minister said he met an altogether different person on a Sunday night a few months later, when, at Dick Lord's invitation, I returned to speak to the Rush Creek youth group.

"Kevin had a sense of peace about him that night that most people don't have," Derek recalled in an interview with Tim Madigan. "He had been paralyzed for twenty-five years by then, and to have that peace and to express the love that he expressed . . . He had just a powerful presence, and every time I've been around him since, there is that sense that he is complete."

The night of my visit to Rush Creek, I was both excited and nervous as I rolled into the room full of teenagers and several adults. It was the same room at the church where my parents had been teaching dance lessons to the youth group on that fateful afternoon a quarter of a century before. Dick quieted the room.

"I want to introduce you to a friend of mine, someone you might have heard something about," the pastor said. "I don't know of any other person who has suffered like Kevin Curnutt, but a few weeks ago, he told me some things about his journey that he and I both feel you need to hear."

I smiled and rolled to the front of the room, nodding to an applauding audience. I cleared my throat and began to speak in a quiet voice, pausing often because of my limited lung capacity.

"It was a little over twenty-five years ago, on January 25, 1981. I was thirteen years old, and I had spent the night with my best friend, Trey Shelton, who lived about half a mile west of

Kevin, age four,
in preschool in Lubbock.

Kevin, age ten, on
the soccer field.

Kevin, age ten, on a family trip to San Francisco.

Kevin, age ten, at Universal Studios in Los Angeles.

Trey Shelton. Courtesy of the Shelton family.

Left to right: Jeff Jordan, Trey Shelton (age 14), and Nathan Moore at Gunn Junior High School.

Kelly Curnutt with Kevin at Craig Rehabilitation Hospital in Englewood, Colorado.

Kevin at Red Rock Canyon during a trip to Las Vegas, Nevada.

Kelly Curnutt, Greg Ticknor, and Kevin at The Mirage in Las Vegas, Nevada, in 1994.

From left to right: Kelly Curnutt, Mary Tom Curnutt, René Cowart, Lori Lane, and Kevin, on the night that Kevin and René Cowart met.

Kevin with actress Brittney Powell in Dallas.

Kevin and Jo Dee Krotz after a meal of sushi.

Kevin answering questions after speaking to a youth group. Also pictured is coauthor Tim Madigan.

Former Arlington police officers Tommy Ingram, Ruben Puente, Mike Yantis, and Kevin.

Kevin's parents, Gail and Jerry,
with Kelly Curnutt at Rush Creek Christian Church.

Kevin and coauthor
Tim Madigan.

here. It was a Sunday, Super Bowl Sunday, in fact. It was early afternoon, and we decided to skip the country western dance class right here in this very room, taught to the youth group by my parents. Trey and I already knew how to dance—I was a pretty good dancer, if I do say so myself—so we went riding on a couple of Trey's motorbikes instead.

"We were riding up and down Trey's back driveway, a dirt road through the woods which ended at Bowen, about a hundred yards from the church. A neighbor, who was apparently insane, thought we were making too much noise and shot and killed Trey and shot me in the head."

I heard quiet gasps in the room and saw some of the young people put their hands to their faces.

"I don't remember anything about getting shot. One minute I was riding the motorbike, and the next minute I'm struggling to wake up from a coma two weeks later. I was very confused, to say the least. I couldn't figure out what had happened. Then someone me told what had happened, but they didn't say anything about Trey. I had a lot of visitors, and I remember being very hurt that Trey never came to see me. Finally, they told me why, that Trey had died. I was devastated, of course."

I saw Derek listening from the back of the room.

"You could look around and see tears in the eyes of most people," he remembered. "It's just a sad, sad story. But what really struck me that night was . . . I mean, these were kids that I normally had to pull out of the trees and keep from climbing on the church roof. They were just so still, listening with rapt attention, wanting to hear every word Kevin had to say."

"When this happened," I explained, "I would often ask myself, 'Why did this happen to me? What did I do to deserve this? I've been a fairly decent guy. I never did anything that bad, so why me?' I never got an answer to those questions. Sure, some people would say, 'God works in mysterious ways,' or, 'God has a plan, even if we don't know what it is.' But would God be so cruel?

"Over the years, through the various struggles of rehab and coming to terms with my injury and my life, I've tried to work out my own beliefs by constantly questioning things. I never want to take someone's word for it, especially about the important questions of life. 'Because I say so,' 'That's just the way it is,' or 'Because that's what I was taught, so it must be right' were never good enough for me, which drove my parents crazy."

Several adults in the room squirmed at what I said next: I didn't believe in heaven, hell, or an afterlife of any kind. To me, God was not an all-powerful supreme being who bestowed peace and prosperity on some people but condemned others to tragedy and misfortune.

"I don't really think you could even call me a Christian," I conceded.

Derek was among those taken aback.

"It sounded like Kevin had chosen something like Buddhism, and it surprised me that was what Dick wanted the youth to hear," he later recalled.

But then I began to talk about what I *did* believe.

"I believe God is the love in every person's heart. God is not 'out there,' but rather God is 'in here.' I believe our task in life is not to worship a supreme being. What we need to worship and grow is love itself, through loving and cherishing one another, through acts of kindness, and trying to better understand one another.

"How do I know this? I've experienced it, very recently in fact. Not too long ago, just last fall, I didn't think there was much point to my life, being stuck in this wheelchair until the day I died, a burden to others, not being able to do things that other people take for granted. But when I got to my lowest point, I came across a few books that told me there might be a different way of looking at things. One was written by a man who survived the Holocaust and had managed to stay positive despite what he had seen and experienced.

"So I read those books, and thought about them deeply, and tried to change painful thoughts to loving ones, and very gradually, almost imperceptibly at first, the darkness began to go away. Eventually, after a period of several months, I knew the darkness was completely gone, and my heart was filled with this love I'm talking about. You could call it a miracle, I suppose. Now I think I understand the teachings of Jesus, which were about love. I don't necessarily worship the messenger, but I do worship that message, which always comes back to love.

"I realize my beliefs are different from many of yours, and not a traditional understanding of God and Jesus, but when you really think about it, they are quite simple and straightforward. If that love exists within me, I know it exists within you. What can be simpler than the idea that love lives within each and every person, and that every person can bring that love to the surface of their being?"

It was the most powerful force in the universe, this love, stronger than any tragedy or evil, I said. Love allowed people to rise above the most difficult challenges and difficulties that are a part of every human journey. I felt like I was living proof.

"One of the things I've learned recently is that everyone has a choice about how he or she will react to any situation, even to something as horrible as what happened to me. For a long time, I didn't think that was possible. How could I choose to be happy and loving, stuck in a wheelchair for the rest of my life? But here I am tonight.

"No matter what happens, no matter what is 'done' to you, you can choose how you respond. We can't control what other people do or how other people act, just like I had no control over that insane man with the gun. But I *can* control how I respond to what he did. Hopefully, I will respond with love and dignity. Every last thing can be taken away from you, but you'll always have the freedom to choose how you'll respond to any given situation. That man I spoke about earlier, the one who survived the Holocaust, called it the last of the human freedoms.

"Finally, when you realize that love is really who you are, you start to ask a different question about life. The right question is not 'What do we expect from life,' but 'What does life expect from us?' To me, the answer is pretty simple. Life is about living, and living is about loving. Love is the salvation of man, the ultimate truth. *Love* is a verb, something you do. No matter what life brings your way, you can love, freely and without condition."

I smiled when I finished. When the applause died down, the young people and many adults came forward to embrace me.

"He was a stranger to them, and most of the time with teenagers there is a tentativeness about getting close or speaking to someone they are not familiar with," Derek remembered. "It was the opposite that night. They all wanted to be close to Kevin and hear anything else he had to say. I worried that he would feel claustrophobic the way they were crowding around him."

I asked them if they had any questions for me. One teenager asked me if I had forgiven the shooter.

"Yes, I just feel pity for him," I said. "To be that angry and that bitter, to come out and shoot to kill two little boys, it must have been awful to live that way."

"Did you hear your friend get shot?"

I said I didn't.

"Were you wearing a helmet?"

I said I wasn't.

"Did you ever wonder why your friend had died and you survived?"

"That bothered me for a long time," I said. "But I've learned not to question why things happen, good or bad."

"Before you found the love within yourself, what did it feel like?"

"I felt really angry," I said. "Angry at God. Angry at everybody and everything. But gradually I realized there was no future in anger."

As the teenagers lingered, many of them kneeling by my wheelchair, one wanted to be sure.

"After everything you've been through, your message is love?"

I smiled.

"Yes, exactly," I said.

CHAPTER SEVEN

Strange as it would seem, I never suffered nightmares about the day I was shot. I remembered little of it, for one thing. Another possible explanation, at least during the patterning years of my adolescence and young adulthood, was exhaustion. After the relentless daily exertions, when the lights were turned off in my bedroom at night, I was too tired to dream.

Later it could be said that I warded off any night terrors through force of will. After my liberation from rehab, I was quite single-minded in my determination to focus on the next road trip or the next night out with my friends, not on the tragedy that had defined my life for so long. It wasn't until the dark times of 2005 that I began to realize the residue of what had happened was still with me and was unavoidable, and was made even more painful by how little I actually knew about the details of the crime that left me paralyzed. My depression had deepened, and angry thoughts had filled my tortured mind, and I had only a vague idea of what Richard Tiedemann even looked like—I didn't even have a face upon which to focus my hate.

Then came the spring of 2006, when the hate, the rage, and the depression had been swept away. One by-product of my new inner peace was the sense of wonder, not regret, with which I came to view my life. I found myself becoming grateful for my life instead of being bitter about it. I began to see it as the remarkable journey that it was. I realized very few people had experienced what I had and had lived to tell about it. Yet it was clear, as I reflected upon my past, that there was an important chapter of my story that was missing. If I was to know and to appreciate the whole story of Kevin, there was a blank spot that needed to be filled in.

My first step was to contact the Arlington Police Department, which I did in the late spring of 2006. I made several phone calls and inquiries, and eventually I obtained the email address of the victim services coordinator for the APD, a woman named Derrelynn Perryman. I then emailed her and asked her if it would be possible for me to see any and all information—police reports, photographs, et cetera—the police department had from a crime that had occurred in 1981. I told her that I had been one of the victims. Derrelynn replied that it was material to which I was entitled to by law.

"Tell me a little more about it, and we'll go from there," Derrelynn said.

I could tell she was surprised when she learned about what had happened on Super Bowl Sunday a quarter of a century before. In 1981 Derrelynn was a senior in high school in nearby Fort Worth and had not heard about the shooting at the time it occurred. In an interview with Tim Madigan, she said that after she received my email reply, she started asking around the department about the crime. She had no trouble finding veteran officers who remembered one of the worst crimes in the history of the Dallas–Fort Worth suburb.

I had told her that I wanted to see everything, so Derrelynn dug out all the incident reports and photographs from musty boxes in the storage area. She studied the material herself before meeting me to be prepared for the emotional impact it might have on me.

"I don't ever want to excavate someone's intense memories without being sure that we've got a plan in place in case it gets really hard for them," she said years later.

There was certainly reason for concern in this case. I had lived through a horrible crime, and then, as a quadriplegic, I had been forced to confront the reminders of it every day since. I had been just thirteen years old when I was ambushed and shot off my dirt bike, saved only by the prompt action of responding police officers and paramedics. I would be a man of thirty-eight on the day of our upcoming appointment. Derrelynn said she thought she might meet someone who was anxious, fearful, and bitter; however, she later said, she did not expect the person who rolled into the police department in his motorized wheelchair with a smile on his face.

"Later on, after our time together that day, I was certainly curious," she remembered years later. "We spent hours together at the police department, and the sense of calm never left him. I watched him closely, looking for signs that it was too much.

Occasionally, his eyes grew a bit teary, and his expression was somber. But he was so well prepared. I will always remember that calm.

"Not that I thought he wasn't reacting genuinely, that he was in denial or anything like that. It was clear his peace came from deep within. I just wanted to know where his resilience was coming from. Kevin and I became friends that day. We later had conversations about his spiritual journey. That's when I came to know who he was, what he had done, and how he had done it. I learned about the growth that had brought him to that point. It was awesome."

On the day of our meeting, we sat down in a nondescript room at the police department, where Derrelynn had stacked the reports and photographs on a table. Before we began, she reminded me that I could stop at any point if I began to feel overwhelmed. I nodded. She placed the first report in front of me.

> ARLINGTON POLICE DEPARTMENT
> DETECTIVE DIVISION
> INVESTIGATIVE REPORT
> Offense/Incident: Death investigation
> Complainant/Suspect: Richard Wade Tiedemann
> Detective assigned: Ruben Puente
> Date: 1-25-1981
> [Tiedemann] was shot and killed during a gun battle

> with Arlington Police Department Tactical Unit officers. Hours before the confrontation with police, Tiedemann shot to death 14-year-old Ralph Shelton as Shelton was riding his motorcycle on a lot adjacent to the south side of Tiedemann's property. Tiedemann also shot 13-year-old Kevin Curnutt.

Most of the subsequent reports were similar to that one, tersely written and brief. I studied page after page of hand-drawn diagrams of the crime scene that showed the location of Tiedemann's home, outbuildings, the riding trail, and trees that were riddled with bullets. In the diagrams, Trey and I were represented by stick figures. Then Derrelynn gave me the report of Mike Yantis, the first police officer on the scene. On that Sunday, Yantis was notified at 3:29 p.m. of the possible sniper situation. He arrived at the scene two minutes later.

In his carefully printed narrative, written in black ink, Yantis described meeting the witness, Kathy Strong, who pointed to where Trey was lying, and to the white house that could be seen through the trees.

"The suspect had gone back inside and was still in there, as far as they knew," Yantis wrote.

With his weapon drawn and one eye on the white house, Yantis scanned the woods and spotted me for the first time. As I read, I tried to picture it through the eyes of the young officer.

> I observed a white male with blond hair lying on a dirt trail which runs east and west through the wooded area. The

> boy was lying just to the north of the trail and a red dirt bike was lying partially on top of him. Approximately ten feet away, to the southwest of [the boy] was a yellow dirt bike lying in the dirt trail. I observed a second [victim] lying face up in the grass on the north side of the trail. [He] was approximately fifteen yards east of the yellow dirt bike and lying about five feet off the road. He was wearing brown shoes, blue jeans, and a maroon shirt and had dark brown hair. The first [victim] was still moving and the second was lying still and appeared to be dead. I found a gate in the fence. I opened the gate and proceeded down the dirt road to the [boy] lying in the grass north of the roadway. I knelt by [him] and observed blood on the back of his head. I checked for vital signs but could find none. He was a gray color, was not breathing and appeared to be dead.

I felt my cheeks flush as I paused to imagine the scene, two boys sprawled and bleeding in the shade of the beautiful winter afternoon, me clinging to life, Trey's youthful exuberance already snuffed out. I thought about the laughs we had shared on the football field and on those trips to cutting horse competitions. I remembered our roughhousing in my bedroom just the night before. Then this. It was hard to believe those things could have occurred in the same world. Then I thought of Officer Yantis, who was just a young guy himself. He must have been scared and shocked, but reading his report, learning about what he did, I was so grateful he was there, and grateful to the other officers who showed up and saved my life.

Yantis went on to describe how detectives Tommy Ingram and Ruben Puente had screeched up on Bowen at about the same time as the ambulance. Yantis was assigned to cover the gunman's house while the detectives came up with a plan to get me on a gurney and on my way to the hospital. Then Yantis wrote about the bewildering end to it all.

> As the [tactical] officers got in position, I observed the front door of the house open and a subject walk out of the house, across the upper porch, down the steps, across the lower porch and across the yard to a garage. [He] was a white male with dark hair, approximately, 5′10″, wearing blue pants and a maroon shirt. [He] matched the description of the suspect which was broadcast earlier. [He] entered the garage and stayed inside about one minute. He then walked out and walked to the back of the garage, then walked back toward the house the way he came.
>
> As he was walking back toward the house, I observed what appeared to be a rifle or a shotgun in the subject's right hand held along his leg. It is my opinion that [he] was unaware or unconcerned about our presence until he saw an officer and opened fire. I base this on the unconcerned manner in which he first exited the house and the way he walked toward the garage. [He] walked with his head down and seemed in no way excited or upset.
>
> When [he] reached his lower porch, he suddenly raised the gun waist high and fired. The officers began returning fire. The subject fell as if he was hit and began screaming

> and he continued to scream as the officers stopped firing. The subject crawled across the porch up the steps and into the house shutting the door behind him.
>
> After it was confirmed that the subject had reentered his house, an attempt was made to talk the subject out. When [he] refused to reply, tactical officers fired six or seven rounds of gas into the house through the north windows. The north end of the house began to burn and fill with smoke. Suddenly, the front door opened and a [man] came from the house. I was unable to distinguish [his] features as it was now dark and he was backlit by the fire.
>
> [He] lunged out the door, crossed the porch, went down the steps to the lower porch. At this point I could no longer see [him], but could only detect motion. I think that the subject fell or lay down on the lower porch and began to fire again from a prone position as I could see muzzle flashes close to the ground. Tactical officers again returned fire and suddenly the subject raised up and slumped over against the porch steps.

Feelings washed over me. Anger was not one of them. As I was reading that day, I just felt a deep sadness, and not just for the two boys who were the stick figures in those police diagrams. I felt sad for Tiedemann too. What kind of mental illness or inner agony could drive a person to do what he did? It was all such a waste.

After I read over the police reports, it was time for me to view the photographs. Derrelynn followed a protocol for reviewing crime scene photographs with people like me. She started with the most innocuous first, working up to the most graphic and gut wrenching. She described the content of each photograph so that I would have an idea of what was coming. That day with me, she began with aerial shots of the rural area where it happened: trees, a smattering of rooftops, and gravel roads.

Then:

A white house seen through thick brush.

A gravel driveway leading to the house.

Curtains dangling from shot-out windows.

Bullet holes in worn brown paneling in Richard Tiedemann's living room.

A statue of an eagle atop a bookcase filled with textbooks on science and economics.

A toy soldier standing at attention in a corner, next to an old desk.

Technical drawings on the desk.

Crushed eyeglasses lying amid shattered window glass on the floor.

A wooden-handled pump shotgun leaning against a wall.

A blue box of long-range shotgun shells.

That was jarring, seeing the pictures of the shotgun used to kill Trey and nearly kill me. Derrelynn warned me the final pictures would be more difficult.

A long smear of blood across the front porch.

A red dirt bike, on its side in the leaves.

A yellow dirt bike lying beneath a spindly tree.

A dark pool of blood at the place on the trail where I had fallen.

That was very surreal. I could imagine myself, lying there with the blood gushing from my head, clinging to life as Trey lay dead a few feet away. Derrelynn showed me the final images from that terrible day.

Tiedemann lying spread eagle in the leaves and dirt, his blue jeans and maroon shirt soaked in blood.

The killer's bullet-riddled head, his dark mustache on a face covered in blood, mouth open, vacant eyes staring into the night.

Then the body of Trey, lying in the leaves.

I did not look away. That was not Trey. I loved and missed my friend, but he was not in those pictures. Trey was gone. Derrelynn and I visited quietly after I had looked at the last of the photographs.

"I just wanted to make sure he was okay to go home," she remembered. "I wanted to help him prepare to go back to his real life after seeing this stuff. He was going to continue to process it, and I asked if he had someone he could talk to. I told him that sometimes there is a physiological reaction, changes in appetite or sleep, and to be prepared if that were to happen. But given the serenity I observed, I thought that unlikely."

I told Derrelynn how much I appreciated her kindness and compassion. And I said I was glad I had come. I felt a sense of completion. We spoke again of the officers who were there that winter day in 1981, and she asked if I would like to speak to one or more of them. I told her that I would love to, and she said she would be more than happy to help me with that.

Detectives Tommy Ingram and Ruben Puente went on to long and distinguished careers with the Arlington Police Department, as well as other police departments and organizations, but of the thousands of cases they handled over the years, none would remain more vivid or haunting than the one that occurred on Super Bowl Sunday in 1981. Both often wondered about the boy they found clinging to life that day in the woods.

"Over the years I would periodically call Jerry, Kevin's dad, to find out how Kevin was doing," Ruben remembered years later in an interview with Tim Madigan. "I knew Kevin collected baseball caps. I eventually went to work in security for Major League Baseball, so I got Kevin a cap. But emotionally I had a hard time seeing him. Even talking about him right now is a little difficult."

Tommy never forgot an emotional meeting with my parents a few days after the shooting.

"Kevin's mother asked if she could hug me," he told Tim Madigan. "So she held me in an embrace and said, 'Thank you for saving my child.' Here I am, a guy in my midtwenties, dealing with this. It was a little traumatic for everyone. I was used to working homicide and seeing bad guys get shot and killed, not kids. It had a lasting impact on everybody there. It was just one of those tragedies of life and tragedies of your career that you hope you never see again. But I'll always remember the profound thank-you they gave us that day and the way they treated me personally. I would have done it again a million times for those people."

In the years to come, Tommy followed media accounts about my rehab program and checked in occasionally with my parents.

"I never wanted to intrude but was always available if they ever wanted to talk about anything," Tommy recalled.

He told Tim Madigan that he was delighted when Derrelynn called him in the spring of 2006. By then Tommy was the new police chief in Colleyville, a suburb of Fort Worth. When Derrelynn mentioned my name, she didn't have to explain any further. One afternoon a short time later, Sedgwich Washington drove me to the Colleyville police station. After twenty-five years, Tommy and I were reunited.

As we sat in Ingram's office, I remember how I struggled to find adequate words to convey my gratitude to the officers for risking their lives to save mine. I finally settled with what was genuine and heartfelt: "Thank you for saving my life, Tommy." Tommy said he wished they could have done more. Then I asked him to start at the beginning, to describe the chain of events as he remembered them from that January afternoon. To the officer, it was like it had all happened the day before.

Finding us in the woods.

Fears of the gunman in the house a short distance away.

The plan to shield the paramedics and get me to the ambulance.

The standoff with Tiedemann and its violent end.

Tommy told me that he and Ruben had been assigned to conduct the follow-up investigation.

"No, there never were any answers," Tommy remembered years later in the interview with Tim Madigan. "He [Tiedemann] was quite a loner. He appeared very well educated and highly intelligent, but lacking in social skills, kind of a hermit. When we went through his house, he had some of the work-related stuff, aerospace drawings. Some of his drawings were just incredible. I remember thinking, 'How could someone this incredibly intelligent do something like this?' The only thing we could ever come up with was the annoyance from the sound of the dirt bikes just caused him to flip out. That wasn't uncommon, but to do that was way off the beam."

But our discussion of the shooting and its aftermath lasted just a few minutes. For the rest of the hours we spent together, we just talked about life. Tommy said he understood why it was so important to know the details of what had happened, because his own father had been murdered when he was six years old. When Tommy tried to inquire about it as an adult, he was told the case files had burned in a courthouse fire.

Then, on the corner of Tommy's desk, I noticed a copy of *The 7 Habits of Highly Effective People*. The book was dog-eared and full of yellow Post-it Notes marking his favorite passages.

"We got to talking about that," Tommy told Madigan. "I'm a prolific reader and that this is one of the best books I've read, just kind of a guide for life. That was the way I tried to do my job, live my life, and treat people. I told Kevin that there were times when I struggled, and I would go back to that book and look at things. It sat at the end of my desk. It lived there, and there was rarely a week that I didn't thumb through it and look at some excerpt I had highlighted, to the point that pages were literally falling out."

I shared my own experience with Stephen Covey's book.

"Kevin said, 'That book saved my life,'" Tommy remembered. "That's what he told me. I thought it was incredibly ironic, strangely coincidental, and quite unique."

We would both later remember that afternoon we spent together as one of the most meaningful of our lives. Given the history we shared and our common outlook on life, I felt an almost familial connection to the officer. I think Tommy felt the same.

"I'm sitting there and looking at someone who has every reason in the world to be profoundly bitter, but who isn't," he remembered. "Someone who has every right to be mad at the world, but isn't. Someone who could have just withdrawn into a dark place and never come out, but didn't. Not only was he living, but he was living well.

"He had been to the lowest point that a soul can be, and he had climbed out of the hole, and he was living and thriving. That was the best part of it. I didn't think he was going to make it to the hospital, but here he is, a bright and intelligent young man. Yeah, he had challenges, but he had overcome them.

"Working homicide, you didn't get many happy outcomes. Almost never. Bad things happened at the worst possible times, and they usually got worse. And it was a long, long road for Kevin, a journey with a lot of rocks and potholes. But he had come up and hit that smooth water. It was just incredible to see how well he had done."

CHAPTER EIGHT

My spiritual awakening came more or less out of the blue, without any significant religious experience or belief, so maybe it was understandable for me to wonder in the beginning if I had somehow lost my mind. Was this new inner peace I felt authentic and permanent? Or was it a particularly convincing delusion that could fall apart at any time? Had others experienced the same expansive love and light, or was I a kind of cosmic freak? As was typical with me, I was determined to find out.

I did not think it likely that the answers I sought were to come from the Christianity of my childhood, which seemed to me too rigid and doctrinal. I turned instead to what, by Western standards at least, were unconventional sources. I sought out and devoured books and videos on ancient wisdom, from the mythology teachings of Joseph Campbell to Tibetan Buddhism and Zen; from the sacred text of Hinduism, the Bhagavad Gita, to the Tao Te Ching of premodern China. I learned in the process that transformations such as mine, though rare, have been a part of the human experience since ancient times, that rapture and enlightenment have been written about and celebrated for millennia. It was a relief to learn that I was not making these things up or going crazy or living in my own little fantasy world. These things were real and identifiable, and confirming this through other sources gave me a great sense of peace. What was happening to me was real. It gave me the confidence to say, "This is my home. This is where I belong. And this is where I will remain. Living in the world, but not being bound by it."

Early in my spiritual education, I came across the writings of a teacher named Ram Dass. The former Harvard professor, born and raised with the name Richard Alpert, had abandoned a life of American privilege in the 1960s to explore his own experience of the transcendent. After years of study with his guru in India, Ram Dass returned to the United States and published the 1971 spiritual classic *Be Here Now*. The book was an introduction to Eastern thought and spirituality for thousands of Westerners, and I read it eagerly, as I did another title by Ram Dass, a meditation guide titled *Journey of Awakening*. Both of these books contain countless passages that could have been dictated from my own heart.

"Though the numbers are proportionally few, many thousands of us have, through discipline and persistence, arrived at a view of our lives that is open, clear, and detached," Ram Dass wrote in *Journey of Awakening*.*

> In this new space we have a lightness, an ease in carrying out our daily lives, an ability to keep a certain sense of humor

---

* From JOURNEY OF AWAKENING by Ram Dass. Published by Penguin Random House.

> about our predicaments. We find that because of the quietness of our minds it's easier to relate to acquaintances, to family, to employers, to friends . . .
>
> We begin to feel a little bit like gods on earth, for where we see sadness and suffering around us, we are able to empathize and still feel lightness and joy. It's as if the world is made for our delight, and even our own troubles become a source of amusement. When we look one another in the eye there is clarity and honesty. We have a certain degree of inner peace. Many of us never thought possible this feeling of equanimity, fullness, and delight in life. We have a sense of self-acceptance, spaciousness, and fullness in the moment that makes each day enough. In many ways it seems like liberation.
>
> As I look around at people I know who have been working intensely on themselves for some time, there is a dramatic change. I see beings who were initially preoccupied with their melodramas, whose bodies were their enemies and who were attached to spiritual melodrama, now bright, clear, and strong.

Melodrama was an apt word. My life had been defined by unspeakable violence, followed by years of anguish and struggle, then life-threatening despair and a body that truly did seem like an enemy. And then I discovered the light and the peace within me. In the end, I did indeed feel "bright, clear, and strong."

"When the student is ready, the teacher appears." The Eastern maxim has become a cliché of sorts, but I think I'm living proof of the veracity of that statement. Stephen Covey and Viktor Frankl had thrown lifelines to me in my season of suicidal despair. Then, each in their own time, like-minded souls joined my path, introducing me to teachings that deepened the understanding of my bliss. One of them was a Hollywood actress named Brittney Powell, whose own period of soul-searching and spiritual exploration began with a marital breakup.

I met Brittney on MySpace through the sister of a friend of mine in the mid-2000s. Over the years, and especially in the beginning of our friendship, Brittney and I had very deep conversations about spirituality, life, and the human experience. She has one of the most beautiful souls I have ever come across. Without her, I don't know if I would be the man I am today. I will be forever grateful to her for that.

It was Brittney who shared with me a line from one of Buddhism's Prajnaparamita (in Sanskrit, "perfection of transcendent wisdom") sutras: "Not just the illumined wise ones but every single being in the interconnected world is a dweller in the boundless infinity of love." That term, "boundless infinity of love," became an inspiration and a touchstone of my life, the name of my website and my email address (kevin@boundlessinfinity.net).

Our friendship developed over email and on social media but eventually came to include an in-person visit when Brittney came to Texas for a movie shoot. She invited me to the Dallas set and then to a cast party. We also had the opportunity to share a couple of meals together, during which she helped me with my meal.

"Just tell me what the rules are," Brittney told me. "Do you want me to offer to feed you, or do you want to ask me to help you? I don't want to overstep. I don't want to make you uncomfortable. I don't know the standard procedure."

I remember grinning at her.

"If you want to offer me something, feel free," I said. "Nothing is going to offend me. You take a bite of food, and then you give me a bite of food. It's pretty simple."

During our time together, we talked about many things, among them more about how I became a quadriplegic.

"You didn't hear sadness in his voice," Brittney remembered in an interview with Tim Madigan. "You didn't hear anger or pain. It was like, 'This is just what happened. So be it.' I was exponentially more impressed that he wasn't holding that anger. It would be one thing if it would have been a car accident, but it wasn't. It was a human being who laid in wait just because they were making noise, like children do.

"I just wanted to turn into an angel and swoop Kevin up," Brittney continued. "I've had more time process it now, but when you first hear that, your jaw drops because you're in awe. It's a scary story. You're just, like, numb, but fuming and don't know where to put it. But luckily, the person that it happened to is calm, matter-of-fact. It helps to bring you back to your center."

Our conversations, especially in the beginning, inevitably turned to our shared spiritual path and the healing that helped us to endure and transcend the tragedies and challenges of life. It was Brittney who suggested I read *Be Here Now*, by Ram Dass.

"I told him it was a hippy-dippy book, but I loved it, and I hope he loved it too," Powell remembered. "I just started throwing out names of books that I loved, and the next thing I know, he's reading them. I'm like, 'Dang, he means it.'"

But I wasn't content to just read the books. I would sit with the latest spiritual book open on my lap for hour after hour, contemplating the meaning of every line, every word. When I came to a passage that spoke to me, and there were literally thousands of them over the course of my early study, I would dictate it onto a page on my computer screen. Then I would look up at the screen to see if there were any typos or if I had misspelled any words. It was important I get it right, because these words seemed sacred. I continued to do it line by line, page after page. It certainly wasn't easy, but I understood that these spiritual classics were not like the novels I was reading for entertainment, something I could read and then quickly forget. I needed to know these teachings and go over them again and again so I could learn them thoroughly and completely. And that's exactly what I did. Otherwise, what was the point? The whole reason for taking these notes and going over these teachings again and again was so that I could internalize them so they would become a part of me. And I think they have.

On page 80 of *Be Here Now*, Ram Dass quoted Vivekananda, a nineteenth-century Indian mystic: "The human mind is like that monkey, incessantly active by its own nature, then it becomes drunk with the wine of desire, thus increasing its turbulence. After desire takes possession comes the sting of the scorpion of jealousy at the success of others, and last of all, the demon of pride enters the mind, making it think itself of all importance."*

I also love this passage a little further on, on page 90:

> Ask yourself: Where am I?
>
> Answer: Here.
>
> Ask yourself: What time is it?
>
> Answer: Now.
>
> Say it until you can hear it.
>
> For specific periods of time focus your thoughts in the present.
>
> *Don't think about the future.*
>
> *Just be here now.*
>
> *Don't think about the past.*
>
> *Just be here now.*

The Tibetan Book of Living and Dying, by Sogyal Rinpoche, became a surprise bestseller in the United States when it was published in 1992. Rinpoche, who had been born in Tibet and raised by monks and Buddhist teachers in that Himalayan nation, came to England to teach and study in the early 1970s.

---

* Ram Dass, Be Here Now (Santa Fe, New Mexico: Hanuman Foundation, 1971).

His book, like *Be Here Now*, became a spiritual bridge between East and West, a thorough but accessible primer on Tibetan Buddhism (Vajrayana Buddhism, the form of Buddhism practiced by the Dalai Lama). It was also one of the books most enthusiastically recommended to me by Brittney Powell.

To the shock and dismay of so many readers and admirers, Sogyal Rinpoche was forced to retire a few years before his death in 2019, when credible accusations came to light that he sexually abused some of his followers. But when I studied the book in 2008, I found *The Tibetan Book of Living and Dying* one of the most impactful and illuminating texts of my spiritual study. I now recognize Rinpoche's serious temporal flaws, but I also see the beauty, depth, and sacred truths of his work. I would highly recommend its study for anyone interested in spirituality in general, and Tibetan Buddhism in particular.

For just one example, I recognized my own experience in Sogyal Rinpoche's description of the spiritual realm foundational to every human life, "the sky-like, deathless nature of mind and the ground of our transient, mortal nature." The Tibetan term was *rigpa*, "a primordial, pure, pristine awareness that is at once intelligent, cognizant, radiant, and always awake. It could be said to be the knowledge of knowledge itself."*

"Saints and mystics throughout history have adorned their realizations with different names and given them different faces

---

* From The Tibetan Book of Living and Dying by Sogyal Rinpoche. Copyright © 1993 by Rigpa Fellowship. Used by permission of HarperCollins Publishers.

and interpretations, but what they are all fundamentally experiencing is the essential nature of the mind," Sogyal Rinpoche wrote. "Christians and Jews call it 'God'; Hindus call it 'the Self,' 'Shiva,' 'Brahman,' and 'Vishnu'; Sufi mystics name it 'the Hidden Essence'; and Buddhists call it 'Buddha nature.' At the heart of all religions is the certainty that there is a fundamental truth, and that this life is a sacred opportunity to evolve and realize it."

The Tibetan Book of Living and Dying also introduced me to Buddhist concepts that many Westerners still find exotic and even threatening, such as nonattachment (ceasing to grasp at things), impermanence, and nonduality. To me, it's just common sense. *The Tibetan Book of Living and Dying*, and Buddhism in general, showed me the folly of attempting to achieve security and deny the inevitability of death by seeking out and clinging to objects and ideas in the material world. The problem is, the material world is forever changing and impermanent by nature.

On page 25, Rinpoche wrote:

> One of the chief reasons we have so much anguish and difficulty facing death is that we ignore the truth of impermanence. We so desperately want everything to continue as it is that we have to believe that things will always stay the same. But this is only make-believe . . . the rickety foundation on which we construct our lives . . .
>
> In our minds changes always equal loss and suffering. And if they come, we try to anesthetize ourselves as far as possible. We assume, stubbornly and unquestioningly, that

permanence provides security and impermanence does not. But, in fact, impermanence is like some of the people we meet in the life—difficult and disturbing at first, but on deeper acquaintance far friendlier and less unnerving than we could have imagined.

On page 33, he explained further:

Grasping is the source of all of our problems. Since impermanence to us spells anguish, we grasp onto things desperately, even though all things change. We are terrified of letting go, terrified, in fact, of living at all, *since learning to live is learning to let go*. And this is the tragedy and the irony of our struggle to hold on: not only is it impossible, but it brings us the very pain we are seeking to avoid.

The intention behind grasping may not in itself be bad; there's nothing wrong with the desire to be happy, but what we grasp onto is by nature ungraspable.

And on page 35, he discussed the benefits of nonattachment:

How, then, can we work to overcome attachment? Only by realizing its impermanent nature; this realization slowly releases us from its grip. We come to glimpse what the masters say the true attitude toward change can be: as if we were the sky looking at the clouds passing by . . .

As we try to follow the masters' advice and are slowly released from attachment, a great compassion is released in

> us. The clouds of grasping part and disperse, and the sun of our true compassionate heart shines out. It is then that we begin, in our deepest self, to taste the elating truth of these words by William Blake:
>
> *He who binds to himself a joy,*
> *Does the winged life destroy;*
> *He who kisses the joy as it flies,*
> *Lives in eternity's sunrise.*

In his book, Sogyal Rinpoche both affirmed my own experience of the transcendent and encouraged me to explore it fully, which too few in the West dare to do. Three passages have been particularly meaningful to me. These are found on pages 51, 52, and 54, respectively:

> I think we do, sometimes, half understand these glimpses, but modern culture gives us no context or framework in which to comprehend them. Worse still, rather than encouraging us to explore these glimpses more deeply and discover where they spring from, we are told in both obvious and subtle ways to shut them out. We know that no one will take us seriously if we try to share them. So we ignore what could be really the most revealing experiences of our lives, if only we understood them. This is perhaps the darkest and most disturbing aspect of modern civilization—its ignorance and repression of who we really are.

> Looking in will require of us great subtlety and great courage—nothing less than a complete shift in our attitude to life and to the mind. We are so addicted to looking outside ourselves that we have lost access to our inner being almost completely. We are terrified to look inward, because our culture has given us no idea of what we will find. We may even think that if we do we will be in danger of madness. This is one of the last and most powerful ploys of ego to prevent us discovering our real nature.

> The wonder of this promise [regarding enlightenment] is that it's something not exotic, not fantastic, not for an elite, but for all of humanity; and when we realize it, the masters tell us, it is unexpectedly ordinary. Spiritual truth is not something elaborate and esoteric, it is in fact profound common sense. When you realize the nature of mind, layers of confusion peel away. You don't actually "become" a buddha, you simply cease, slowly, to being deluded. And being a buddha is not being some omnipotent spiritual superman, but becoming at last a true human being.

Meditation was the way to examine and expand this radiant inner nature, Sogyal Rinpoche wrote. "The gift of learning to meditate is the greatest gift you can give yourself in this life. For it is only through meditation that you can undertake the journey to discover your true nature, and so find the stability and confidence you will need to live, and die, well. Meditation is the road to enlightenment."

Since my early reading of Stephen Covey and Viktor Frankl, I had practiced my own sort of contemplation, thinking deeply about the concepts I had been introduced to, challenging them from one perspective or another. Sogyal Rinpoche was suggesting something quite different: making a conscious attempt to *not* think, because one's swirling, fear-based, ego-centered thoughts were the main barrier between a person and their experiencing their own transcendent nature. On page 60, he wrote:

> The purpose of meditation is to awaken in us the sky-like nature of mind, and to introduce us to that which we really are, our unchanging pure awareness, which underlies the whole of life and death.
>
> In the stillness and silence of meditation, we glimpse and return to that deep inner nature that we have so long ago lost sight of amidst the busyness and distraction of our minds. Isn't it extraordinary that our minds cannot stay still for longer than a few moments without grasping after distraction?
>
> We are fragmented into so many different aspects. We don't know who we really are, or what aspects of ourselves we should identify with or believe in. So many contradictory voices, dictates, and feelings fight for control over our inner lives that we find ourselves scattered everywhere, in all directions, leaving nobody at home.
>
> Meditation, then, is bringing the mind home.

He expanded on the concept of meditation on page 80:

> What we have to learn, in both meditation and in life, is to be free of attachment to the good experiences and free of aversion to the negative ones.
>
> Whatever method you use, drop it or let it dissolve on its own, when you find you have arrived naturally at a state of alert, expansive, and vibrant peace. Then continue to remain there quietly, undistracted, without necessarily using any particular method. The method has already achieved its purpose. However, if you do stray or become distracted, then return to whatever technique is most appropriate to call you back.
>
> The real glory of meditation lies not in any method but in its continual living experience of presence, in its bliss, clarity, peace, and, most important of all, complete absence of grasping. The diminishing of grasping in yourself is a sign that you are becoming freer of yourself. And the more you experience this freedom, the clearer the sign that the ego and the hopes and fears that keep it alive are dissolving, and the closer you will come to the infinitely generous "wisdom that realizes egolessness." When you live in that wisdom home, you'll no longer find a barrier between "I" and "you," "this" and "that," "inside" and "outside"; you'll have come, finally, to your true home, the state of nonduality.

At first I was somewhat reluctant to meditate. Sogyal Rinpoche—and the other masters I have read since—had said so much about the benefits of meditation. But it all seemed so strange, so different. How could an exercise of "not thinking" be so special as to transform my life? It seemed too good to be true. But I was drawn to the promise of peace and equanimity, and so I finally started to meditate.

I began to meditate for thirty minutes or more every day, initially experimenting with the advanced methods from *The Tibetan Book of Living and Dying*, including the use of mantras. Over time, however, my practice became much simpler. In a lecture to a graduate social work class in the fall of 2020, a student asked me to describe my method of meditation.

"First of all, I sit and I relax all my muscles, from the tips of my toes and my fingertips, all through my body up to my neck and head, concentrating on letting go of all the tension built up in those muscles," I replied. "While I'm relaxing all my muscles, I take slow, deep breaths, inhaling slowly and deeply, and then exhaling slowly and deeply. I do that for a few minutes. I then try to shut out all external influences, concentrating on my breath, following my breath—just breathing in as slowly and as deeply as I can and breathing out as slowly and as deeply as I can, and I do that repeatedly, while trying not to become attached to my thoughts as they arise.

"I often picture myself sitting next to a stream in the lotus position, observing the leaves floating down the stream. The leaves are my thoughts. But instead of attaching myself to the leaves, or my thoughts, I just let the leaves float on down the stream."

The goal of meditation is to quiet our minds. Our thoughts, left unchecked, seem to chase each other around in our minds and can't seem to settle themselves down. Meditation is not so much to erase all thoughts as it is to quietly and compassionately settle your mind and your thoughts. It doesn't matter what "method" you use, whether focusing on an invisible point in your mind, a recitation of a prayer or a mantra, or the sublime sound of a beating drum. If you can quiet your mind, that's all that matters.

Using the simple process described above, I was able to quiet my mind. Without the barrier of thoughts, I could more easily return to that sacred place within myself where the ego and the challenges of the material world did not intrude.

While meditating, the primary focus of your practice should be to expand your awareness of the present moment by being mindful. Mindful of what is going on in your mind (hence, mindful); the thoughts, conflicting emotions, and the positive and negative thought patterns afflicting your mind. The key to mindfulness is realizing we have control of our thoughts, and we ourselves condition our mind by the thoughts we think. If we condition ourselves to think negative, unwholesome thoughts, that's what we will think. But if we condition ourselves to think positive, compassionate, loving thoughts, *that* is what we will think.

Meditation takes work and practice though. Be patient with yourself, and be compassionate with yourself. It will take time, and just like working out your physical body, learning how to meditate is a gradual process. After all, you wouldn't expect a single trip to the gym to put you into the perfect physical condition.

Meditation allowed me to access that place within myself that was open, expansive, and limitless. The place within myself that was full of peace, of contentment, and of love. Boundless love, where all people and all things are one. Where all separation is revealed as the illusion that it is. I could now see that all things are one. There was no more duality.

Above all, meditation is not a method for escaping reality; meditation is a method for understanding the true nature of reality.

The contemplation I had come upon through Covey and Frankl was more externalized. I was trying to deal with suffering caused by the outside world. When I started meditating, and did it more and more, I felt the energy coming from the inside. Meditation seemed to open up a whole new dimension. It allowed me to more easily shed my ego and what I had once thought of as myself in the external world. It taught me that the true reality was not the external body and the material world; it was the internal consciousness.

I also realized that if I could do it, anyone could, and that we are all connected in that way. We share that same consciousness, billions of times over. Realizing that, I felt even more connected to all the other souls in the universe. Through meditation, we can see the external world for what it is, touch this consciousness that is universal and in all people, and connect in an extremely deep way.

Jo Dee Krotz had taken up art as therapy after a divorce, and she found she had a unique aptitude for it. Within a few years, hundreds of boutiques across the United States were featuring her T-shirt and apparel designs. But when a partnership with a friend soured, she lost her business, her home, and the friendship.

"I remember calling Kevin," Jo Dee remembered years later in an interview with Tim Madigan. "I was losing everything I identified with. I said, 'Just when I felt like I had lost everything, I realized I still had some more to lose. I still had my freedom. I still had my choices. I still had my gratitude. I still had my ability to look at the whole situation as a new beginning in a series of endings. I could still map out something past this. There were some new paths for me to adventure into.' He responded something like, 'Yes, that's exactly right.'"

Jo Dee and I had met when she was in high school and her Girl Scout group volunteered to help with my patterning program. On her Friday afternoon team, Jo Dee was put in charge of moving my left hand.

"I was on the floor with him. He was in a harness system in a crawl position," she remembered. "He would attempt to move forward, and everything was very measured, and the concentration was very intense. Just watching the determination on his face . . . You were allowed to witness this struggle, to absorb his fight."

We lost touch for a while when Jo Dee left for college, but we eventually reconnected on social media.

"I remember one time I had this horrible cold, and I reached out to him," Jo Dee said in the interview with Tim. "I said, 'Here I am, feeling all sorry for myself with Kleenexes all around me, and I started thinking about you and what happened to you.' We started to connect on this deeper level because he had experienced the struggle I had witnessed. He was open to sharing about it and listening. I remember asking him, 'How do you blow your nose when you have a cold? What do you go through when that happens? What do you do when your leg itches, and you can't scratch it?' Do you know what he said? 'It just itches.'

"We talked about puddles of pain, about going into pain and coming out the other side," she said. "A lot of people, they just want to hear the highlights. They don't want to hear the struggle, the pain you go through. There's a line in a Dan Fogelberg song, 'There's a light in the depths of your darkness.' I was always searching for little messages like that. I would chat with him about how we got to where we are. We would talk about being full in your heart."

First broadcast in 1988, *The Power of Myth*, a six-part series of conversations between host Bill Moyers and mythologist Joseph Campbell, became one of the most-watched programs in the history of American public television. Many years later, Jo Dee happened across the DVDs of *The Power of Myth* while browsing for spiritual material in a bookstore. She bought a set of the DVDs and watched them with growing fascination. When Campbell described the central story of mythology, the hero's journey, Jo Dee said she thought of me.

"For me, it was about a flawed human going into the darkness and learning to carve out a path that didn't look like anybody else's," she said. "I can almost visualize someone on a horse going into a dark forest, and that's how I saw Kevin too. But he had come out of the darkness already.

"This may sound cheesy, but I saw an analogy in how his patterning in the physical world had finally come to completion. Joseph Campbell describes the patterns of heroes. Kevin grabbed onto the spiritual pattern of Joseph Campbell's heroes and was able to make out of the spiritual patterning what he couldn't with the physical."

I had not heard of Joseph Campbell until Jo Dee told me about him over a meal of sushi. That night she started emailing me clip after clip of excerpts from *The Power of Myth* on YouTube. I bought the set of DVDs for myself, watching them repeatedly and taking careful notes. One exchange struck the deepest chord:

> Moyers: So who would have been in these early elementary cultures, as you call them, the equivalent of the poets today?
>
> Joseph Campbell: The shaman. The shaman is the person who has in his late childhood, early youth, could be male or female had a—an overwhelming psychological experience that turns them totally inward. The whole unconscious has opened up and they have fallen into it. And it's been described many, many times and it occurs all the way from Siberia right through the Americas down to Tierra del Fuego. It's a kind of schizophrenic crack-up, the shaman experience.
>
> Moyers: What kind of experience?
>
> Joseph Campbell: Dying and resurrecting, you know, being on the brink of death and coming back. You actually

experience the death experience. People who have very deep dreams. Dream is a great source of the spirit. And then people who in the woods have had mystical encounters.

Moyers: Let me try to be specific about that. The shaman becomes some person in a society who is drawn by experience from the normal world into the world of the gifted?

Joseph Campbell: That's right.

Moyers: Most of us think of shaman as a magician, but they play a much more important role than simply being a trickster?

Joseph Campbell: They are playing a role that the priesthood plays in our society.

Moyers: These are the first priests?

Joseph Campbell: There's a major difference as I see it between the shaman and a priest. A priest is a functionary of a social sort. The society worships certain deities in a certain way, and the priest becomes ordained as the functionary to carry on that ritual, and the deity to whom he is devoted is the deity that was there before he came along. The shaman's powers are symbolized in familiars, deities of his own personal experience, and his authority comes out of a psychological experience, not a social ordination. Do you understand what I mean?

Moyers: And the one who had this psychological experience, this traumatic experience, this ecstasy, would become the interpreter for others of things not seen?

Joseph Campbell: He would become the interpreter of a heritage of mythological life you might say, yes.

> Moyers: And ecstasy was a part of it, very often, in the shamanic tradition?
>
> Joseph Campbell: It is ecstasy, there's no doubt about it.*

Again, I recognized much of what Campbell described. I, too, had fallen into a deeper level of consciousness, and like the shaman I was determined to share that experience and interpret it for others, to spread the news that another dimension was there for the taking. And yes, I thought, it was ecstasy.

In another seminal work, Joseph Campbell outlined the path of the hero in mythological traditions in *The Hero with a Thousand Faces*. On page 18, Campbell wrote:

> Furthermore, we have not even to risk the adventure alone, for the heroes of all time have gone before us. The labyrinth is thoroughly known. We have only to follow the thread of the hero path, and where we had thought to find an abomination, we shall find a god. And where we had thought to slay another, we shall slay ourselves. Where we had thought to travel outward, we will come to the center of our own existence. And where we had thought to be alone, we will be with all the world.†

---

* From Joseph Campbell and The Power of Myth with Bill Moyers, courtesy of Alvin H. Perlmutter, Inc. Video available at: https://www.kinolorber.com/product/the-power-of-myth

† From Joseph Campbell's *The Hero with a Thousand Faces* Copyright © Joseph Campbell Foundation (jcf.org) 2008. Used with permission.

On page 188, he discussed the hero's journey as well as his return:

> The hero adventures out of the land we know into darkness; there accomplishes his adventure, or again is simply lost to us, imprisoned, or in danger; and his return is described as a coming back out of that yonder zone. Nevertheless—and here is a great key to the understanding of myth and symbol—the two kingdoms are actually one. The realm of the gods is a forgotten dimension of the world we know. And the exploration of that dimension, either willingly or unwillingly, is the whole sense of the deed of the hero.*

That is exactly what I felt. I had been thrust, most unwillingly, into an exploration of the darkness of the world and of my soul. In that exploration, I had finally come to terms with my situation and my soul, and I felt an overwhelming sense of peace because of it. And now that I have returned from the darkness, I've made it my life's goal to share these lessons I've learned about life, about sorrow, about joy, and about the true experience of being human.

On page 204, Campbell wrote, "The meaning is very clear: It is the meaning of all religious practice. The individual, through prolonged psychological disciplines, gives up completely all attachment to his personal limitations, idiosyncrasies, hopes and

---

* From Joseph Campbell's *The Hero with a Thousand Faces* Copyright © Joseph Campbell Foundation (jcf.org) 2008. Used with permission.

fears, no longer resists the self-annihilation that is prerequisite to rebirth in the realization of truth, and so becomes ripe, at last, for the great at-one-ment. His personal ambitions being totally dissolved, he no longer tries to live but willingly relaxes to whatever may come to pass in him; he becomes, that is to say, an anonymity."* And on page 222, he explained, "The adventure of the hero represents the moment in his life when he achieved illumination—the nuclear moment when, while still alive, he found and opened the road to the light beyond the dark walls of our living death."†

In *A Joseph Campbell Companion: Reflections on the Art of Living*, Campbell poignantly discussed how to live joyfully in a world often filled with sorrow (page 119): "The field of time is the field of sorrow. 'All life is sorrowful.' And it is. If you try to correct the sorrows, all you do is shift them somewhere else. Life is sorrowful. How do you live with that? You realize the eternal within yourself. You disengage, and yet, reengage. You—and here's the beautiful formula—'participate with joy in the sorrows of the world.' You play the game. It hurts, but you know that you have found the place that is transcendent of injury and fulfillments. You are there, and that's it."‡

---

* From Joseph Campbell's *The Hero with a Thousand Faces* Copyright © Joseph Campbell Foundation (jcf.org) 2008. Used with permission.

† From Joseph Campbell's *The Hero with a Thousand Faces* Copyright © Joseph Campbell Foundation (jcf.org) 2008. Used with permission.

‡ From *A Joseph Campbell Companion: Reflections on the Art of Living*, by Joseph Campbell Foundation, 2011. Ebook. Used with Permission.

I now recognize the eternal within myself, and with that I have finally learned to "participate with joy in the sorrows of the world." And yes, sometimes it hurts. But it is indeed a "place that is transcendent of injury and fulfillments." And I am there, and that's it.

CHAPTER NINE

On an autumn night several years after my spiritual awakening, I was put to a dramatic and unexpected test. I had come down with a chest cold as my parents were getting ready to leave for a week of vacation, but my sniffles and a bit of a cough were certainly no reason for them to change their plans. After all, it was just a cold. I had been through this many times in the past few decades, and I knew what to expect: a runny nose, congestion, and a slight headache, but nothing that wouldn't go away in a few days. It was definitely something to be aware of in my condition, but nothing very serious. Kelly would stay with me until my parents got back from their much-deserved getaway to Colorado.

But a couple of nights after they left, with Kelly asleep in the next room, I was jerked awake by . . . something. It took me only a few moments to realize something was terribly wrong. I could not breathe. As much as I tried to inhale, something seemed to be caught in my throat or in my lungs, preventing any inhalation. I choked and was desperate for a breath, but it would not come. And without a breath, I could not call out for help. My oxygen-deprived body began to panic, desperately clawing for breath, violently spasming as I sought to inhale, but without any result. I lay helplessly in bed, quietly suffocating.

"Well, this is it," I thought. "I'm dying, and there's nothing at all I can do about it."

But then I realized something very curious that was *not* happening. I was not in the least bit afraid. Instead, I was able to observe the desperate state of my body from a place of inner stillness. It was a strange sensation. My physical body was doing what a body does when it is threatened. But inside, in my deeper consciousness, I was thinking, "Well, if this is the end, I'm ready to go. Not that I necessarily want to die, but I don't really have any strong feelings about it one way or another. If it happens, if this is the night, I'm ready." I had accepted the inevitability of death, the impermanence of all existence, and I was totally at peace with it.

Even under those extreme circumstances, I was able to distinguish between the two realms: my body and my inner consciousness, my true being. I didn't have to look for it. It was just there. I had been contemplating and meditating long enough that I knew what it was. I had been living out of that place of light and of love for several years now, and had long since separated how "I" was from how my body was. That night my body may have been on the knife edge between life and death, but my inner consciousness, my true being, what I had finally come to think of as "myself," was still living a transcendent life, as it always would. Whether in life or in death, it would always live on, in some form.

After all these years, I'm still not sure if my inner peace helped to save my life, calming my body enough to allow my shallow breaths to come. It may be that my body would have eventually calmed itself without it. But whatever the case, I was able to calm myself enough to take several shallow breaths and then to call out for help. I went to the doctor the next day and was diagnosed with a case of pneumonia.

At the moment it happened, as I struggled to breathe and felt certain I would not survive for much longer, I was conscious of an overwhelming sense of peace within me. Moreover, I immediately recognized what it was, the great achievement I had stumbled upon. No thoughts of the past or of the future entered my mind. There was only the inner stillness focused on the present moment that I had come to know, that place of light and of love.

What I had come to know, I could share with others, and it could save lives and transform them for the betterment of humanity. Even in the direst of circumstances, there was no fear of death in the transcendent realm.

Dick Lord died in 2017 after contracting West Nile virus. He had touched the lives of so many with his kindness, his wisdom, and his ministry. In the days after his death, I reflected on that and recalled with gratitude our shared journey over the years, from the day of my shooting until he fell ill and passed away. Dick was a man of God in the finest sense.

He also played a pivotal role in another important episode in my life. Late in 2009, Dick introduced me to another good friend of his, Tim Madigan, a senior writer at the *Fort Worth Star-Telegram*. Tim and I became close friends and would eventually collaborate on this book. But when we met, Tim had another purpose in mind: proposing what would be a three-part newspaper series about my life. The series, which was published in February 2010, was accompanied by a documentary film produced by the *Star-Telegram*'s Jen Friedberg (now Jen Robin) titled *Worthy*, a reference to the Dostoyevsky quote I had come across in Viktor Frankl's book, *Man's Search for Meaning*: "There is only one thing that I dread: not to be worthy of my sufferings."

The first screening of Jen's film took place on a crisp winter night at Rush Creek Christian Church, a few days after the series was published. The reader response had been overwhelming, but I still couldn't help wondering whether anyone would show up at the church that night. I shouldn't have bothered worrying. The sanctuary was full to the bursting point, with the overflow standing at the back of the room.

That night became a reunion of sorts for so many of the people who had affected my life in a very positive way: the patterning volunteers were scattered among the crowd, the police officers who had saved my life were seated together on the front row, and I was surrounded by my family and my many loving friends. There were also many strangers who had read the articles and were curious to know more. I was deeply humbled and more than a little bit nervous when Dick welcomed everyone and then introduced me. I thanked everyone for coming, and I spoke about my favorite themes: the love and the peace I had found and my desire that others find it too.

Then the lights went down, and my story came to life on the screen. There were photographs of Trey and I as carefree teenagers, shots of grainy old newspaper clippings about the ambush in the woods, aerial photographs of a rural south Arlington, and the pictures of the gunman, his actions, and his demise. But I was most touched by the words of the people whose lives had also been profoundly impacted by the tragedy. Kathy Strong was one of them. She still lived in the same house, the place where she had heard the shots and then tried futilely to warn me about the gunman.

"I think about it all the time," she said while being interviewed in the sunlight just a few feet from where we fell. "I can't get the vision of Trey and Kevin out of my mind. Each day I come out and I look over there. The setting is still the same, and it never goes away. It was as if he [the gunman] was in a trance, and he was holding a gun and he was looking at Trey, as if he was waiting for Trey to get up or move."*

Dick Lord spoke of his lingering amazement that something so evil could have happened just across the street from his church. "We assumed he would die," Dick said, referring to me. Ralph Shelton said that were it not for Tiedemann's death, he might have felt obligated to take it upon himself to avenge

---

* Jen Friedberg, "Worthy," uploaded February 9, 2010, video, 23:30, https://www.youtube.com/watch?v=PlH9dapT1Cc.

Trey's murder. Officer Mike Yantis described coming upon Trey in the woods, and then finding me. "I could still hear the other boy [Kevin] breathing," he said. "One of the things that sticks in my mind is that I told him, 'Hang in there. I'll be right back with you. I'm going to get some help.'" My parents spoke of the surreal horror of the early hours and days after the shooting, and their gratitude to the police officers and doctors and nurses who saved my life.

A video clip of the patterning years showed me trying to move forward inch by inch. A second clip was from the barbecue place on the night in 1996 where I said goodbye to so many of those who stayed with me during those difficult years of rehab. Finally, the film told of my deliverance from suicidal despair into the light.

"In all of my contemplation and my meditation, I kept feeling there was something within myself that was the place where I wanted to be," I said in the documentary. "It's something that originated inside of me, and I understand now that if I strip away all of what I think of as myself, that is God. What is inside of me, beyond self, is God, and what is inside of everyone, beyond self, beyond ego, is God. I just hope to share lessons about what is inside each and every one of us, how much our potential is."

It occurred to me that night, and it still does, that my victory over darkness was not just mine alone. It is shared by the people in that documentary and so many more. No one finds their way to the light alone. Together we made sure love, kindness, and compassion would have the final word. And it has become my chosen mission to deliver that message.

"I admire him. I think he's a hero," Kathy Strong said in the video, her voice quivering with emotion. "He's been a fantastic example because of his essence and his spirit. I know he's a strong individual. I just want him to know that I've never forgotten it, and that I pray for him, every day."

It seemed fitting that Dick Lord would have the final word.

"All of us can learn from him what it means to be a free human being," my friend said. Speaking as if he were me, Dick said, "'I am not determined by my genes, my environment, by other people outside of me. But I am a transcendent and wondrous person who can stand off and look at my life and make decisions about who I will be in that situation.' For so many of us, we're so impressed by what we do and what we achieve and what we possess. And to see Kevin . . . he doesn't possess anything except a very calm soul inside, and that's really what we are all wanting to achieve."

Thank you, my friend, for saying what I didn't have the words for.

Another friend of mine, Chad Duncan, had worked for fourteen years as a teacher of children with special needs, a job he loved and had a special knack for, especially when it came to calming a troubled student. In February 2011, when he was thirty-eight years old, he woke up one morning almost totally blind. Literally overnight, a rare degenerative disorder had permanently taken his eyesight.

When he was no longer able to teach, he enrolled in the graduate social work class of my friend Derrelynn Perryman. In a recent interview with Tim Madigan, Chad spoke of his experiences:

"I was struggling. Gravity just drew me down. I beat myself up for being blind. I beat myself up for interactions in which people were unintentionally cruel. For some reason I felt shame about that. I would apologize to people. I turned all of these things inward, because somehow I felt responsible for being blind, and I felt a responsibility to not let it outwardly show that it was affecting me. Call it perfectionism, but I had to keep that stiff upper lip. It wasn't working.

"I told Derrelynn that I thought I was experiencing symptoms of depression. She is such a compassionate person, and the material she was teaching was just so full of empathy and thoughtfulness. So she was a safe person for me. And she was the one who introduced me to Kevin. Derrelynn said he was one of the wisest people she knew. She shared a little bit of his history, but she didn't tell me why he was wise. She didn't give me the essence of Kevin. I think she wanted him to do that.

"Most of the communication between Kevin and me was by email. I explained a little of what I had gone through and what I was feeling. I had been able to drive and live a normal life and do all these different things. Now all of that was gone. I said to Kevin, 'I feel so isolated, and I have all these emotions. What do I do with these emotions?' He said he didn't allow what happened to his body to dictate what he thought or felt. I'm like, 'What? Don't they have to be connected?' But they don't.

"He wasn't trying to be profound, but he is profound. He didn't know he was mentoring me. He was just being Kevin. He didn't say, 'Here's the answer.' He said, 'Here is what I found, or here is one way to approach it.' I never felt like he was talking down to me. But it was like, 'Whew!' I'll never forget the day, a while after we met, that Derrelynn asked the two of us to present to her class. I talked about working as a social worker with a disability, what it was like for me to adjust. Then Kevin shared. He just laid out in front of these young people that when he was first adjusting, he kept saying, 'Why me? Why me?' But as he learned to meditate, as he learned to read and gain control of and understand his emotions, he came to the point where he started saying, 'Why not me?' I wrote to him the next day and told him, 'Man, you just dropped some Zen bombs on every one of us yesterday.' He said something like, 'Thank you.' Thinking about that still rocks my world.

"Back when we first met, I asked him where I should start, and he recommended reading Viktor Frankl's book *Man's Search for Meaning*. I listened to that book for the first time on the way to getting my guide dog in Michigan. I was up there for twenty days with this new dog, and we'd walk in this little park area. I'd be listening to that book, where Frankl was talking about finding beauty in life in even the worst circumstances, and when I was out with that dog, I started to see it too.

"Kevin was also the one who suggested meditation. I had heard about meditation for a long time, but when I understood what it had done for him, I knew I needed it too. I was certain I was doing it wrong when I started, and I couldn't help but wonder, 'What am I going to get from this?' I tried it for ten minutes at first. I couldn't count two breaths before I had a random thought. But I found out that ten minutes was okay, so I thought, 'Let's do fifteen.' Then, 'I wonder what twenty minutes would be like?' Eventually, I could count to ten without a thought. And when a thought would come, I wouldn't beat myself up over it like I did about everything else before. I would just say, 'Fantastic, let's start over.' That started to carry over into life. It used to be that certain interactions would pull me down. But now, when I would feel vulnerable, I would know it was just a feeling and let it go like a cloud in the sky. I didn't have to try to hide the vulnerability or hide the shame.

"Kevin brought me there. Since I got the dog I've lost 160 pounds. I walk a daily 5K and meditate every day before work. When I'm out walking, handing my trust over to this furry beast, I find myself asking, 'Why not me?' This is where I need to be. This is what I need to be doing. I'm made for this. I can do this. When I meditate, a deep calm comes over me.

"More days than not, I am at peace with not being able to see. Most people know what it's like to have driven a truck and all of these other things. But how many know what it's like to walk with a guide dog, to run with a guide dog. Not many. If it weren't for Kevin, I don't think I would have walked down the paths that I did. Read the things that I did. That's the beauty of Kevin."

Years ago, my friend and coauthor, Tim Madigan, published a book about his friendship with Fred Rogers, the icon of children's television. Tim's book, *I'm Proud of You*, told the story of how Mr. Rogers mentored Tim through his own dark night of the soul, a time of depression and despair of the sort I think we all experience at one time or another in our lives. The book also told the story of how the life of Tim's brother, Steve, was transformed by terminal lung cancer.

Before his diagnosis in the fall of 1998, Steve had been consumed with fear, anger, and bitterness. But something changed the moment he received the grim medical news. "I've never been more scared in my life," Steve told Tim. "But in some ways, I've never been more peaceful either. It's not about the cancer but the good that I can make come out of it."

The next two years were agonizing. Eventually, in the summer of 2000, the tumor wrapped itself around Steve's spinal cord and left him paralyzed from the chest down. Married and the father of two young boys, he continued to fight his disease, but he was also the embodiment of peace and wisdom, savoring his first sip of coffee in the morning and the song of a cardinal outside his window. Through his illness, he had touched that light within.

"Steve is teaching us all now," Fred Rogers told Tim.

About two weeks before Steve's death in August 2000, his large family gathered around his hospital bed in the living room of his home in Davenport, Iowa.

"The good Lord has a plan for us all," Steve said that day. "I have accepted my challenge. I wouldn't give it back. Nobody can have it. It's mine, and God knows I'm up for it. We're on a ship going one way, and sometimes it gets a little rough, but we're all in it together, by God. Let's just teach. If we don't teach, all of this crap has been for naught. We can't waste this, because it sucks. But if we can all learn to teach a little better—"

"And love a little stronger," Steve's sister, Terri, interjected.

"By God, every minute has been worth it; every second of it," Steve said. "But if we don't, then it will all go for naught, and we can't let that happen. Does everybody agree?"

The above passage resonates deeply within me. Though I do not fear death, I do live with a certain urgency, a keen desire to share my story to the fullest extent possible while I'm still around to do so. As Steve said, anything less would be a waste. That is the purpose of this book.

I write this in the first few days of 2021, after one of the most difficult years in recent human history. Because of the pandemic and political and societal discord, suffering has been visited upon every corner of the globe. But I can't help but think that so much of the pain in the world is unnecessary, the result of the urges of human ego and a lack of understanding about what is most true of our existence. So many people are lost. I want to help them find their way because I, too, was lost, feeling entitled to my bitterness and despair, oblivious to the fact I was looking at everything in the wrong way.

I will never know why Trey and I rode into the crosshairs of Richard Tiedemann that day so long ago, just like I will never know why, just days before I planned to take my own life, I would decide to have my mother pull down the book by Stephen Covey, and a much different journey would begin for me. I am fine with not knowing, completely comfortable with the mystery. The only thing that matters is what I do with today, with this moment. The present moment is now my friend because I can experience this often crazy world from a place of peace and of love and of light. I have heard the "song of the universe." The worst suffering life has to offer can be overcome. If I can do it, anyone can. That is my message. And I intend to share that message for the rest of my days.

I'll leave you with this, from the first talk I gave to Derrelynn Perryman's students back in 2015. When I finished speaking, a young woman asked me if, after having done all this spiritual work over the years, I had achieved closure. I had never considered that before. After thinking about it for a few moments, it occurred to me that what I had found was not closure but an opening: an opening of my heart and of my spirit, one wide enough to take in all the world and all its people, to love them all, no matter what. My wish is that you find that opening too.

AFTERWORD: THE TAO OF KEVIN

The following are excerpts of my ideas, things I've shared on social media and other correspondence, various short essays I've written, and my poor attempts at poetry. Please forgive me for the latter!

First and foremost, I'm comfortable with the mystery of the spirit and existence. Many people, and I include myself in this as well, oftentimes feel a need to explain *everything*. Curiosity, and the need to find out about the world in which we live, is something we as human beings are born with.

However, when we feel a need to have an answer for everything, even (and especially) those things we don't fully understand, we sometimes trip over our own arrogance. We've got to be comfortable with accepting the fact that sometimes we simply do not know something. That's the mystery of the universe. And I'm totally comfortable and at peace with my not knowing.

I am love. But my purpose is not to show you that I am love; it is to show you that *you* are love as well.

I am fortunate to know what joy and humor are. They are my constant companions in the journey of life!

I didn't start out to help other people; I started out to save myself. But in saving myself, I found that I could save others. Saving yourself is the prime means of saving and helping others.

Wherever I look, the joy of life surrounds me.

Half of the battle is just showing up.

Love as a Light

Love is like a beam of light, shining in the darkness,
illuminating those whom we love.
Most people choose to see themselves as a flashlight,
shining their love in one direction and then another,
and at times turning their light off altogether.
A few choose to see themselves as the sun, sending out love in all directions,
at all times, never asking who, or why, or asking anything in return.

Joy and bliss are not an accident. Joy and bliss are intended. You must learn to cultivate joy by realizing and manifesting your bliss. And remember: Your bliss is *your* bliss. Not anyone else's. But you must work at it, and learn to grow and cultivate your joy and bliss. Only by doing this will you create true happiness in your life.

The light shines from within each of us, and because we are so infinitely different, the light within us shines in infinite ways. But yet we are the same, and we are *one*.

Counting my blessings is like trying to count all the stars in the sky.

I come from nothing, and I will end as nothing, but it's what I do in between those two points that matters.

Come Home

Come home,
To that wonderful space which is love,
Realize,
That the door is open, ever open.

Come home,
To the truth, the truth that is plain to see.
Realize,
We are all one, in this world and beyond.

Come home,
To the place where you belong.
Realize,
We all belong there, we all are there.

Come home,
To the place in your soul where peace and happiness reside.
Realize,
They are always there, waiting for you.

Come home,
To a world of love,
Realize,
It's there, within your heart.

Come home.

Your best teacher is within you.

God is just a reference, a metaphor, for the transcendent.

Think of the top of the mountain as the transcendent, that which transcends words, thoughts, or ideas. People often refer to this transcendence as God, although it is beyond any description or idea of God. Religion (any mythological tradition) is like the different paths leading to the top of the mountain, to the transcendent. From any perspective, one can only see the path that is visible to them. But if one is on the other side of the mountain, the path leading to the top of the mountain, to the transcendent, is a totally different path. All the paths to the top of the mountain lead to the same place.

I went looking for God, but the search led me home.

Throughout my childhood and early adulthood, I pretty much took for it granted that a myth was something that wasn't true. Perhaps it was folklore, or an ancient religion, or a primitive belief system. One thing it was *not* was true. It was something to be joked about or scoffed at. Whereas "religion" was *serious*! However, I now see that mythological traditions/religions all point to the same thing: the transcendent.

Regarding religion and the mythological tradition, as I now see it: the purpose of a mythological tradition (a religion) is to enable the individual to connect with and to identify with the transcendent, and for the two to become one. Some people, if not most people, need a mythological tradition in order to see the transcendent. Some people, however, can touch the formless mysteries of the transcendent directly, without the need for a mythological tradition.

The transcendent: that which transcends all thought, all duality, all being and nonbeing. That which *is*.

All mythological traditions point to the transcendent (God, for lack of a better word). Like the spokes of a wheel, they all point to the center; the middle way, the central way, the union of all.

We are taught mythological traditions by our parents and our culture, but that does not make those traditions the only ones out there.

All religions (mythological traditions) are true, from a certain perspective.

The transcendent (what some people call God) is in everything. From nature to outer space to you and to me, it is in everything. The transcendent is not *separate* from the universe; it *is* the universe. It is not some anthropomorphic being *out there*; it is *in here*, in our hearts and in our souls, in our very beings. It is all pervasive and all encompassing. It is beyond all thoughts of duality.

I see the radiant divinity within myself, and that enables me to see the radiant divinity within you and within everything. We seem to be separate, but that's only an illusion caused by the temporal world. We are one. All of us.

I've never felt comfortable with totally supernatural beings or causes. Too much in the way of make-believe and fantasy. It took me many years to fully understand that this was just a way for people to relate to the transcendent. It's not my way, and I had to do much research and much spiritual exploration (and much soul-searching) to discover that the transcendent doesn't *have* to be supernatural and personal. It can be *impersonal*. As in the transcendent is not the *source*, but rather it is the *manifestation* of the divine.

God is within you. God is within you. Let me say that again: God is within you. God is the spirit of love within you. God is the single point of consciousness within your mind. God is not without; God is within. God is not a being, supreme or otherwise. God does not have the form of an old man sitting on a mountaintop or floating in the sky above. God is the formless, shapeless existence at the core of your being.

The body of humanity feels this, but not quite understanding the depths of their soul, many people give this a familiar form: that of a man. A wise and loving man, but a man nonetheless. In other words, they anthropomorphize the transcendent because they do not know how to visualize, contemplate, and understand it otherwise.

The universe created man, and then man created God in his own image.

There are certain qualities, both "good" and "bad," in the mind of man. The "good" aspects, such as goodness, selfless sacrifice, and love, are what we think of as God. The "bad" aspects, such as selfishness, greed, and hate, are what we think of as evil, as Satan. There are no such beings as God or Satan; these are only aspects of our mind and soul, our inner being. This is the mind and soul of man, of the essence of a human being.

I believe God is the love in every man's heart.

Humans are very social creatures. They always have been, and they always will be. That's why we created the idea of "God," a supreme being. Nobody wants to be alone. So that's why people came up with God. The idea of a being, that is.

Humans are also very inquisitive, very curious creatures. Everyone is looking for answers. Ask the parents of any toddler: the thing they say the most (after "no," that is) is "why?" Everyone, from physicists, biologists, geologists, and other scientists to preachers and priests, is trying to answer the big questions: Why are we here? What are we? Are we more than our biological processes? Is there a God? Who is God? *What* is God?

We must go beyond concepts of pairs of opposites. We must go beyond good and evil, right and wrong, God and man, beyond all concepts of duality.

Love. Kindness. Compassion. *That* is my religion.

Everyone has the potential to be Christlike; everyone has the Buddha nature inside them; everyone has the potential to be pure love. One simply has to reach out to grasp that potential.

There are many paths to God.

The Whisper of God

God whispers in my ear,
but the whisper I hear isn't a voice.
It is a whisper of the wholeness of being,
a hint of the oneness.

It speaks of being the leaves of the trees,
the grass of the plains, and the wind which blows in the evening.
I hear it in the stone, and the wood, and the water,
from the flowers that bloom to the clouds above.

It echoes in the newborn's cry and in the last rattle of death,
it speaks to me of life and death, of joy and pain.
I hear it in you, in me, in everyone, and everything,
limitless of time and space.

It speaks not in a single voice from above,
but from infinite whispers within and around us.
It speaks not as the source,
but as the manifestation.

The whisper is only a hint of the oneness,
for that wholeness of being defies understanding.
It is the beautiful song of the universe,
which whispers in my ear.

Cling to nothing, love everything, and be free. That is nirvana.

"A flower falls even though we love it, and a weed grows even though we do not love it."
—Dogen Zenji

This quote by Dogen Zenji, a Zen master of the thirteenth century, is one of my favorite quotes of all time. In fact, I printed it out and had it framed a decade or so ago, and it sits on my bookshelf to this day. I think it exemplifies, in a perfect way, the beauty and simplicity of the lessons of impermanence, nonattachment, and nondualism.

My happiness is not dependent on what happens. My happiness comes from listening to the song of the universe, experiencing what is, and being in direct contact with the transcendent.

I am everything, and I am nothing at all.

Do you see the beauty and the love that is this existence? Give me your hand and walk with me, and I will show it to you.

Fear is just a thought, a whisper in the mind of man. Pay no heed to the whisper, and be free.

I just can't seem to shake this good mood I'm in!

The key to leading a happy life, a contented life, a *liberated* life, is letting go. Letting go of all fears, bitterness, and selfish attachments. Without doing that, we're forever trapped in an endless cycle of pain and cannot move forward to experience the joy of life.

I read the scripture of life, moment by moment.

I hear much talk about heaven, but as the Gospel of Thomas 113 (for those who follow Jesus) states, "The kingdom of the Father is spread upon the earth, but people do not see it." In other words, heaven is right here, right now. One only has to recognize it is here as the eternal moment.

Stillness, the beating of my heart, the silence of eternity, the joy of existence. These are the things that make me happy, that bring a smile to my face.

Life is pain. Life is suffering. If you are going to live in this world, you are going to have pain. But you will also see great wonder and beauty, and if you're lucky, you'll learn to transcend that pain and dwell, as I do, in the boundless infinity of love.

The central point of the universe is within each of us, at the very center of our heart and soul. From that point all love and compassion flow.

I will wait until the waiting is over. Here's the thing about waiting: often when one waits, one gets anxious and impatient, because one is looking ahead and not concentrating on being present in the moment. Rather than waiting, try just being.

Like a Cloud

Like a cloud I drift above the world,
Free of the chains of attachment.

Shining my love upon all below,
I remain in this world but not of it.

Never knowing how long I will last,
I close my eyes and let the moments flow.

For in the eternal moment lies my heart,
Blessed forever by the peace within.

I was born early this morning and will die happily tonight. I will live, laugh, and love all day long and will accept everything that happens with a sense of wonder. And I will do it all again tomorrow.

I believe in the great cycle of life, the wheel of life that is always rotating, taking you up and down and up and down. It is only in the center of the wheel, the hub, that we are balanced, at rest, and at peace.

Life and death are two sides of the same coin. You can't pick up just one side of the coin. You have to value both sides, and everything in between, and cherish them. Death is not the enemy.

Courage usually does not come all at once but a little bit at a time.

My life is not easy. In fact, it's very difficult. But it's my life, and I value and cherish every moment of it, the joys and the sorrows, the good times and the bad. Some people have it "better" that I do, and some people have it "worse." However, life is not a contest. It's an experience, and it's one I find a tremendous amount of joy and happiness in!

I once thought I was bipolar (manic depressive), but then I figured out that I had so much joy and so much sorrow in my life that it was hard to tell the difference. But then I thought, if I could just get rid of the sorrow, I'd have it made!

I think our lives are like a flower in bloom: fleeting and impermanent, but exceedingly beautiful and a wonder to behold.

Right here, right now, this moment is enough.

I choose the middle way.

The Butterfly

If I gave you a butterfly, what would you do with it?

Would you hold it tight, or keep it caged up?
Or would you release it, and let it fly free?

If you let it fly free, what would you do?

Would you regret freeing it?
Or would you cherish its beauty and freedom as it fluttered away?

As it disappeared beyond reach, what would you do?

Would you wait for its return, with longing in your heart?
Or would you smile, and be at peace?

I search for a place of rest within myself. A place of quiet repose from which all action comes forth.

I try to put myself in accord with nature and with my inner consciousness.

In doing something, especially good works, acts of kindness, and acts of love, I try to act without being attached to the results.

I think expanding your consciousness through higher levels of meditation and thought is of the utmost importance. Finding your center, and acting out of your center in all things, is of vital importance.

A person should find their bliss, whatever it is, and follow it with all their being.

When you look at the world around you, you may see much pain, loss, and sorrow, but that is just the foreground of our existence. Look deeper, and you will see that the background of our existence is love, kindness, and compassion. That is where we need to focus our attention. That is where we need to dwell.

The meaning of suffering is to be "worthy" of your suffering. If you can be worthy of that, you are indeed worthy. Sometimes just surviving the suffering is enough to give our lives, and ultimately our suffering, meaning.

To Live in the Moment

What does it mean "to live in the moment"? First and foremost, it means to free ourselves by letting go of our regrets and fears. Oftentimes we clutch these so tightly to ourselves that we can't distinguish them from us. We lose sight of who we are because we can't see past our own fears.

In Buddhism, there is a saying: "There is no past. There is no future. There is only the now."

If we concentrate on the now, we free ourselves of our regrets and recriminations of the past, and our fears and concerns about the future. The result is an inner peace and equanimity, which is the very essence of happiness.

Also, we learn to enjoy and appreciate everything and everyone as its own unique creation, not just what it can "do" for us or how we can gain by it. Not only every person but everything in the universe, including each and every moment in time, has an incomparable beauty that needs to be recognized. We must realize that every second is precious and must be cherished and savored as it passes by. When we become aware of this and take the time to cherish each moment, the sheer wonder of life becomes apparent, and our joy in it becomes ever present.

To live in the moment, we must totally involve ourselves in whatever we are doing at that moment. Whether we are meditating, working on some project, listening to what someone has to say, or simply eating or drinking, we must focus our entire attention on that one thing as if nothing else exists.

We must focus on the process without looking ahead to the result. The result is unimportant. It's the doing that is important. We must become attached to the process itself, not to the result of the process. If we concentrate on the process, doing whatever it is to the best of our ability, the result of that activity becomes inconsequential.

In fact, the result does not even exist. What we perceive as the "result" of an activity is simply an artificial boundary we create between one activity and the next along our journey of life. We never get to a "stopping" point, because the moments never stop. They just go on and on, like an infinite highway. We are blessed to be allowed to travel it, if only for a while.

Indeed, the ephemeral nature of our journey is among the most important reasons why it's essential that we learn to live in the moment. We can never know how long we have in this life, and each moment could be our last. At any time, we could depart this life for whatever lies beyond. Therefore, we must see each and every moment we're given as a priceless gift to be cherished and appreciated.

Live in the moment . . . love in the moment.

Awakening is there for all, but one must not *seek* it. One must prepare the ground for it and let it come as it comes.

Liberation is always a part of us; freedom is always a part of us; enlightenment is always a part of us. All of those are here right now; we just have to realize that they *are* here. To reach enlightenment is to be a realized being. And it's called realized because for all one experiences, learns, suffers, et cetera, one only has to realize it was there to begin with, it's always been there, and it will always be there. Everything we need to know is within us. All we need to do is to realize it.

What is meant by the eternal moment? Eternity is the *depth* of *being*. People often confuse eternity with time, as in lasting a long time or forever. Eternity has nothing to do with time. Think of eternity as having depth rather than length. Therefore, the eternal moment is that moment of being that has infinite depth, which all moments do. And therefore every single moment is the eternal moment.

All the various emotions we feel are just thought patterns. And as they are thought processes of the mind, we can control all these negative mental states. Fear, jealousy, anger, hatred—all of these are just thought patterns. They are simply our thoughts. Being such, they are in our control, and they can be eliminated. It does take work, though!

"All things in all times teach."

—The Flower Ornament Scripture

Whatever the situation, every experience, thought, and action can be a learning experience.

Be in this world but not of it.

Examine yourself, your thoughts, and your emotions. Try to see where they're coming from and leading to. Look at them from all angles, and make every effort to get *behind* them. That will tell you who you are and what you want to become.

Who am I?

I am the Alpha, and I am the Omega,
I am the sky above, and I am the ground below,
I am the evening thunder, and I am the morning rain,
I am pain, and I am joy,
I am you, and I am me,
I am everything, and I am nothing at all.

There's no difference between life and death, so there's no need to rush from one to the other or to choose one over the other. Existence encompasses both your birth and your death and would not be complete without both of them. Life and death are simply two sides of the same coin. You can't have one without the other.

What is the meaning of life? You give life its meaning in the things you do, in the things you say, and by being the person you are. Being the person you are is the only thing you leave behind in this world.

Life is about living, about doing the things you've never done before, interacting with different people, learning different things. And by always doing the above while respecting and loving other people.

Live life, but do it with kindness and compassion toward all, including yourself. Life is not about being someone other than who you are, nor is it about being perfect.

Transformation of consciousness, changing the way you see things and think about things, is what it's all about.

With an Open Heart

In the beginning, I suffered,
Through pain and torment I somehow survived.

Through survival, I learned what strength I had,
For with great effort, I could shrug off all arrows.

The more I sat in stillness, the stronger my armor became,
Until I could laugh at all attempts at injury.

But as I stared in wonder, a blinding flash of truth
Was revealed to me at last:

Not armor nor strength I needed, but greater love and understanding,
For with an open heart, the arrows pass right through me.

The path through pain and difficulty is straight ahead. You cannot go around it. You must go through it to get to the other side.

My main influences have been my parents, Stephen Covey, Viktor Frankl, Joseph Campbell, Ram Dass, Shunryu Suzuki, Sogyal Rinpoche, Maharaji, the Buddha, the Dalai Lama, and Jesus.

I seem to confuse the nurses and doctors I go to see. No matter the pain I'm feeling or what my condition, they always ask me how I'm doing. And I always say *fantastic*! Because I always am. It's not that my body is feeling great; it's that my *being*, my soul, the inner light of my consciousness, is great. I am not my body; I am my soul, my *being*! I try not to confuse the vehicle, my body, with the driver, my *being*, my *soul*. The latter always burns bright. The former is inconsequential.

As I contemplate my life and my accomplishments, I find I have no degrees, no marketable skills, no technical training. I'm only an expert in one thing: the bright shining light that radiates from my soul.

The Lesson of Impermanence

How can death equal happiness?

We need to recognize and to fully appreciate that the nature of things (people, situations, relationships, plants, animals, jobs—everything and everyone, even the universe itself) is ever changing. Everything we'd like to think of as static and unchanging is in fact always changing. Living, growing, dying, progressing, regressing, et cetera. The natural state of things in the universe is impermanence.

If the nature of everything we hold dear and love is impermanence, if everything is dying, shouldn't that lead to hopelessness and despair? No, just the opposite is true. Once we understand the concept of impermanence, several things happen.

First, if everything is always dying, we learn to look at things as such. If you treat the next person you see as if they're dying, as indeed they are, how can you fail to treat that person with anything but compassion? If you treat everyone you see like that, with love and compassion, both you and everyone you meet will benefit.

Furthermore, once we realize that nothing is ever permanent, we begin to understand that it's foolish to try to hold on to things forever. The tighter we try to grip them, the more they slip through our fingers.

Once we understand the need to let go of everything, to stop trying to hold anything in our grip, we release all our fears and bitterness. And if we have truly stopped trying to hold on to anything, why should we fear death? Death is not the end of the world; it is a part of the world.

If we fully understand the truth that is impermanence, we realize that only by letting go of everything, especially our fear of loss, can we embrace the joy of life and find peace and happiness.

Regarding life after death and a soul: Many people want to hang on to life, and therefore they want to think there is a life after death. They want to continue, they want to think there is some continuation, and they think if there is not continuation, life somehow becomes meaningless. But the beauty and purpose of life are like a flower: its purpose is to live and bloom and be beautiful. No one is surprised when it fades and dies. But that's the purpose of life. To live and grow and be beautiful in the soul, and then to pass away.

A Moment of Clarity

Today is the anniversary date of my injury. As I was lying in bed late last night collecting my thoughts before sleep, I was wondering, as I often do on this date, how I should feel and exactly what this day is. Is it a sad day, full of remembrances of pain, suffering, and death? Or is it just another day here in this glorious existence that we call life?

And then in a moment of clarity, it hit me: *it is both*. I no longer have to choose between the two. I now see this day as just another part of the oneness of life. Of the wholeness of existence.

I often talk and teach about nondualism and nonattachment. Nondualism, the concept of not placing everything into one of two categories (good or bad, right or wrong, big or small, etc.), is at the very heart of this. I now see the oneness without having to categorize this day, or any day for that matter, as either good or bad. All it took was taking a step back to look at it from a different perspective.

Nonattachment (and its counterpart, nonaversion), the concept of not relying on things, people, and situations for our happiness, is at the heart of this as well. Nonattachment does *not* mean detached. When you are detached, you are intentionally turning your back on these things, people, and situations. You are not accepting them. Nonattachment, however, means that you do indeed accept them, but you recognize that they have no control over your happiness. And moreover, when you take a step back and see the whole of existence, you see only *one*, not many, and therefore there is nothing to be attached *to*. You simply *are*. I now see that I simply *am*.

In fact, I now see these two concepts are one and the same. They are simply two different ways of expressing the acceptance of the oneness of life, the wholeness of existence. I count myself very fortunate and very blessed to be able to see this, and I am now totally at peace with this day . . . and all the others as well.

—Kevin Curnutt, January 25, 2020

ABOUT THE AUTHORS

Kevin Curnutt was thirteen years old when he was shot off a dirt bike by a troubled recluse. After that terrible day in Arlington, Texas, Kevin spent fifteen excruciating years of physical therapy trying unsuccessfully to regain the use of his arms and legs, and many more years searching for a way out of deepening despair. It was at his lowest moment that he began to look inward for healing. Years of spiritual reading, contemplation, and meditation led him to a profound understanding of the nature of existence and our place in it. He has dedicated his life to spreading the message of love and healing, and to helping people move past their troubles into the peaceful, transcendent realm he has discovered. He lives in his hometown of Arlington, Texas.

Tim Madigan is the *New York Times* bestselling author of *The Burning: The Tulsa Race Massacre of 1921* and *I'm Proud of You: My Friendship With Fred Rogers*, a critically acclaimed memoir. He and his wife, Catherine, live in Texas.